12" limited edition vinyl
OUT NOW!

CHICO HAMILTON
MYSTERIOUS MAIDEN

SOULFEAST REMIXES BY JOAQUIN 'JOE' CLAUSSELL & BRIAN BACCHUS

12" EP
IN STORES NOW!

vinyl & CD EP
COMING SOON!

"Mysterious Maiden"
[LB020/JS10005]

"The Alternative Dimensions of El Chico"
[SF001/JS10006]

AVAILABLE AT:

joyous shout!
www.joyousshout.com
www.myspace.com/chicohamilton

dope jams
www.dopejams.net

SoulFeast
www.soulfeastmusic.com
www.myspace.com/soulfeast

Out Now!

Chico Hamilton
Juniflip CAT # JS10001

Chico Hamilton
Believe CAT # JS10002

Chico Hamilton
6th Avenue Romp CAT # JS10003

Chico Hamilton
Heritage CAT # JS10004

Chico Hamilton
Hamiltonia CAT # JS10005

Catch Foreststorn 'Chico' Hamilton's
In-Store Performances of material from "Hamiltonia"
EXCLUSIVELY @ Borders in 2008!!

foreststorn "chico" hamilton
hear the NEA jazz master
on joyous shout!

2/15 7 PM
Borders Long Island
1260 Old Country Road
Westbury, NY 11590
Tel. 516.683.8700

3/14 7 PM
Borders Baltimore
170 West Ridgely Road, Suite 220
Lutherville, MD 21093
Tel. 410.453.0727

4/18
Borders Albany
59 Wolf Road
Albany, NY 12205
Tel. 518.482.5800

5/16
Borders DC
1801 K Street NW
Washington, DC 20006
Tel. 202.466.4999

6/20
Borders Providence
142 Providence Place
Providence, RI 02903
Tel. 401.270.4801

myspace.com/chicohamilton
joyousshout.com
distributed by redeye

joyous shout!

BORDERS.

iM
INTERDEPENDENT MEDIA

K'NAAN THE DUSTY FOOT PHILOSOPHER
CANIBUS - TANYA MORGAN - J*DAVEY
EYEZON - SHAYA - TRUTHLIVE
WINDIMOTO - SIN

ALL NEW ALBUMS DROPPING IN 2008

TRUTHLIVE
The Unlearning

SHAYA
Fallen Awake

EYEZON & SEAN LANE
A People Like Us

WWW.IMCULTURE.COM

K'NAAN - The Dusty Foot Philosopher CD/DVD

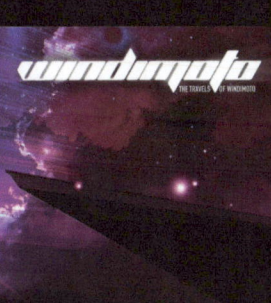

WINDIMOTO
The Travels Of Windimoto

TANYA MORGAN
Moonlighting

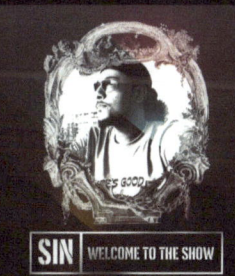

SIN
Welcome To The Show

WWW.IMCULTURE.COM

waxpoetics

LABELS WESTBOUND RECORDS • FANIA • TROJAN • WEST END RECORDS • STONES THROW • NOW-AGAIN • UBIQUITY • LUV N' HAIGHT • DAPTONE • DELICIOUS VINYL • MACKROSOFT • NATURE SOUNDS • NUMERO GROUP • BLOOD & FIRE • QUANNUM PROJECTS • NINJA TUNE ARTISTS FUNKADELIC • ARTHUR RUSSELL • BIZ MARKIE • KOOL G RAP • JVC FORCE • FELA KUTI • GERALDO PINO • HALLELUJAH CHICKEN RUN BAND • SERGE GAINSBOURG • WILD MAGNOLIAS • OHIO PLAYERS • THE PHARAOHS • EL MICHELS AFFAIR • DE LA SOUL • CYMANDE • DIZZY GILLESPIE • PENTANGLE • BADEN POWELL • LUIZ BONFA • ASTRUD GILBERTO • TOM ZE • OS MUTANTES • LEE "SCRATCH" PERRY • BOB MARLEY • BLACK UHURU • DESMOND DEKKER • DENNIS BROWN • BIG YOUTH • EEK-A-MOUSE • GREGORY ISAACS • ISRAEL VIBRATION • YELLOWMAN • RAY BARRETTO • JOE BATAAN • TITO PUENTE • JOE CUBA • EDDIE PALMIERI • MONGO SANTAMARIA • LOUIE RAMIREZ • LEBRON BROTHERS • WILLIE COLON • LA LUPE • CAL TJADER • POETS OF RHYTHM • TOMMY GUERRERO • JIMMY MCGRIFF • EDAN • YO GOTTI • ZIMBABWE LEGIT • SUN RA • ORNETTE COLEMAN • AUGUSTUS PABLO • DILATED PEOPLES • LITTLE BROTHER • SA-RA • BARRINGTON LEVY • DEL THE FUNKY HOMOSAPIEN • RICKEY COLLOWAY • TANYA MORGAN • THE STRANGE FRUIT PROJECT • THE MACKROSOFT • CHEEBACABRA • MAC DRE • MADVILLAIN • YESTERDAY'S NEW QUINTET • QUASIMOTO • LOOTPACK • STARK REALITY • DUDLEY PERKINS • OH NO • WILDCHILD • PERCEE P • J DILLA • L.A. CARNIVAL • THE HELIOCENTRICS • KING TUBBY • THE CONGOS • ORQUESTA HARLOW • QUANTIC • NOSTALGIA 77 • BERNARD PURDIE • DARONDO • GILLES PETERSON • BOB & GENE • SHARON JONES • CHICO HAMILTON • EIGHTBALL & MJG • PEOPLE UNDER THE STAIRS • RZA • BLACK IVORY • NINEY THE OBSERVER • DJ KRUSH • DJ CAM • BILL LASWELL • BAD BRAINS • PRINCE PAUL • PETER TOSH • SLY & ROBBIE • WILLIAM PARKER • NICOLE WILLIS & THE SOUL INVESTIGATORS • THE FREE DESIGN • JACKIE MITTOO • BETTY DAVIS • NEW MASTER SOUNDS • BROTHER AH • O'DONEL LEVY • BLACKALICIOUS • LIFESAVAS • MICKEY & THE SOUL GENERATION • BOOGIE DOWN PRODUCTIONS • DONNA MCGHEE • MC SHAN • MARLEY MARL • ROXANNE SHANTE • RUDY RAY MOORE • 9TH WONDER • LOOSE JOINTS • TAANA GARDNER • PIECES OF PEACE • ORLANDO JULIUS • TONY ALLEN • CLARENCE REID • MF DOOM • CAMP LO • SESSO MATTO • BUSY BEE • THE BUDOS BAND • THE DAKTARIS • SUGARMAN 3 • THE PHARCYDE • TANGERINE DREAM • MAD PROFESSOR • LARRY YOUNG • JAMES MOODY • T A P P E R Z U K I E

○

new digital downloads store & wax poetics website April 1, 2008

THE MOMENTS
"Baby I Want You" *b/w* "Pray for Me"
LIMITED EDITION 7-INCH OUT NOW

EARL ZERO
"Righteous Works"
MARCH

MELVYN PRICE
Rhythm & Blues
MAY

DETROIT SOUL
1962-82 Compilation
SEPTEMBER

12 STAR RECORDS
Disco Rap Compilation
OCTOBER

coming soon on wax poetics records 2008

waxpoetics

№ 27

cover

Front
Grandmaster Flash, circa 1980
photography Lisa Haun/Michael Ochs Archives/Getty Images

Back
Eddie Harris, circa mid-1970s
photography Michael Ochs Archives/Getty Images

contents	*page*
Editor's Letter	15
Re:Discovery	16
In Memoriam	26
Tom Terrell	34
Brownout	46
Blue Note Sampler	48
Hot 8 Brass Band	50
Camp Lo	52
Build an Ark	56
Funky Cuba	60
Mighty Hannibal	70
Eddie Harris	76
Derf Reklaw	90
Newcleus	94
Grandmaster Flash & the Furious Five	102
Chuck Brown	120
S.O.U.L.	132
Jazz Icons	138

errata
Issue 26's Little Beaver photographs were courtesy of Dante Carfagna. In that article, Sam & Dave's Dave Prater was misspelled as Frater. We regret the errors.

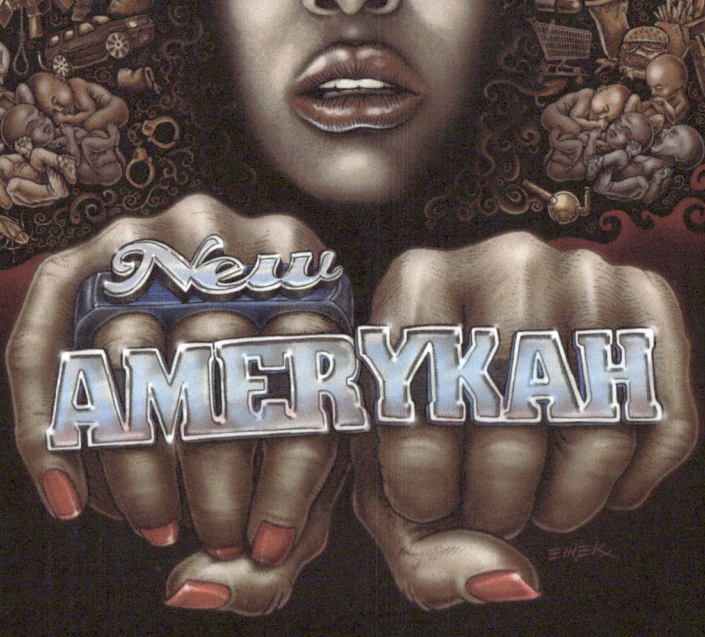

waxpoetics

masthead

Editor-in-Chief
Andre Torres

Editor
Brian DiGenti

Marketing Director
Dennis Coxen

associate editor
Jon Kirby

copy editor
Tom McClure

art director
Freddy Allen Anzures

production designers
Greg DiGenti
Melanie Hendel

production assistant
Kristofer Ríos

advertising sales manager
Michael Coxen

record label manager
Amir Abdullah

online sales manager
Kristofer Ríos

accounts receivable
Connie S. Reale

webmaster
Luis Lucas

interns
Amanda Charnley, Ely Delman, Melanie Hendel, Oskar Mann, Ashley Mui, Kiera Peppers, Billi Richards, Idris Robinson, Greg Winter

contributing editors
Dante Carfagna
John Paul Jones
Andrew Mason
Matt Rogers

contributing writers
Robbie Busch, Seb Carayol, Thomas Sayers Ellis, Ryan Hunn, Jon Kirby, John Kruth, Andrew Mason, Mark McCord, Kristofer Ríos, Matt Rogers, James Steiner, Andy Thomas, Richard Torres, Adam Windmill, Pablo Ellicott Yglesias

contributing photo editor
B+

contributing photographers
B+, Martin Cohen, Michelle Elmore, David Gilder, Tom Terrell

contacts
WAX POETICS, INC.
45 Main Street, Suite 224
Brooklyn, NY 11201
p 866-999-4WAX
p 718-624-5696
f 718-624-5695
info@waxpoetics.com
waxpoetics.com

ADVERTISE
advertise@waxpoetics.com
or call 718-624-5696 x203

SUBSCRIBE
subscribe@waxpoetics.com
waxpoetics.com/subscribe

RETAIL
retail@waxpoetics.com
or contact Melanie Raucci,
Disticor Magazine Distribution
Services, at 631-587-1160
mraucci@disticor.com

CONTRIBUTE
editorial@waxpoetics.com

WAX POETICS IS PRODUCED ON A MACINTOSH USING ADOBE SOFTWARE. PUBLISHED BY WAX POETICS, INC.. PRINTED BY MGM PRINTING GROUP. DISTRIBUTED BY DISTICOR MAGAZINE DISTRIBUTION SERVICES. © 2008 WAX POETICS, INC. ALL RIGHTS RESERVED. UNAUTHORIZED DUPLICATION WITHOUT PRIOR CONSENT IS PROHIBITED. ISSN 1537-8241

RESPECT WORLD WIDE
SCRATCHLIVE

ROCK SOLID DJ SOFTWARE AND HARDWARE. FREEDOM TO HAVE YOUR ENTIRE COLLECTION AT YOUR FINGER TIPS. MIX WITH REAL DECKS. THE TOOL REAL DJS TRUST.

Z TRIP • DJ AM • ROB SWIFT • RONI SIZE • DJ RIZ • DJ VADIM • DJ HAUL & MASON • JOHN TEJADA • JAZZY JEFF • DJ BIG WIZ • A-TRAK • A-SIDES • JAZZY JAY

WWW.SCRATCHLIVE.NET
RANE CORPORATION • USA • 425-355-6000 • WWW.RANE.COM || serato | RANE

A Letter from the Editor-in-Chief

I'm not gonna lie, these past couple of months have been the most trying of my life. In the lab straight through the holidays and into this second month of the year, it got hectic for a minute. But we do what we have to do to survive, and I feel good about where we've arrived. My first son turned four years old a few days ago, and now I'm writing this letter marking the close of Wax Poetics No. 27. It took a minute, but we wanted to set it off in '08 with this joint looking fresh and clean. After six years, we took a look back and decided to switch it up a bit—nothing too drastic, just minding our Ps and Qs.

One thing that we're still paying close attention to is our formula for delivering dope content with each outing. And this issue is no exception. From our inside look at cover artist Grandmaster Flash as things were bubbling early on with the Furious Five, to the complex story of the enigmatic Eddie Harris, we lay it down like no one else. Go-go pioneer Chuck Brown stretches out on being a D.C. legend, while we celebrate the life of fellow D.C. native Tom "The Shutter" Terrell with a eulogy by friend and fellow scribe Richard Torres—complete with a selection of Tom's photos from over the years. Tom had just written our Miles Davis cover story and we consider him fam. Unfortunately, we also mourn the loss of another member of the Wax Poetics family, Joel Dorn. Joel was always there to say a kind word about fellow musicians and producers, many who had recently passed away. They will both be missed. We don't like having to do obituaries at all, but most certainly not with cats so close to our camp.

Repping Brooklyn, we always like to be able to show our own some love. Both with roots in Bed-Stuy, proto techno-rap band Newcleus and beat-head favorite S.O.U.L. represent with their tales of life in music from two distinct eras in the biz. Eddie Harris sideman Derf Reklaw and the soul man Mighty Hannibal further illustrate the sometime harsh realities of the industry. When we add into the mix a little funky Cuba and a taste of new-school brass band, Hot 8, it's clear there's a greater story being told that we're just lucky enough to deliver.

Last year was big for us, but already this one is even better. Back in it to win it, this year will see us getting busy with not only the magazine, books, and records, but working our way into other formats as well. And coming soon, the illest download site on the Internet, hands down. A monster in the making, had to take it back to the lab for a minute and get it right. Bear with us; when it comes, it'll wreck shop. So in the meantime, enjoy the new look, and get ready for another year of slang editorial.

Ridin' with Obama,

Andre Torres

re:Discovery

OPUS SEVEN "Bussle"
SOURCE RECORDS
1979

Like most semi-industrious Southern towns, Winston-Salem, North Carolina, was, in musical terms, doing its thing in the 1970s. Aside from hosting the usual slew of national acts, Winston-Salem was home to nationally recognized artists like the Blenders, the Eliminators, and Odyssey Five. But Opus Seven, previously the Superiors Band, had stuck it out the longest. After a series of popular local releases through the early '70s, Opus Seven used their own money to record a collection of songs with hopes of gaining major-label attention. Meanwhile, in New York City, MCA was entrusting their vice president of marketing, Logan Westbrooks, with a large sum of money to start a subsidiary, which would come to be known as Source Records. After striking gold with his first release, "Bustin' Loose" by Chuck Brown and the Soul Searchers, he would follow suit with "Bussle," the first single by Carolina phenoms Opus Seven.

Recorded at Apogee Studios in Atlanta, Georgia, Opus Seven took a shine to disco, because, as front man Sam Hamlin Jr. explains, "that's what was going on at the time." Regardless, "Bussle" is a four-on-the-floor disco delicacy—chonky horns careen around the voluptuous curves of this dance-floor fable, with the astrological consciousness of Earth, Wind and Fire but the roller-skating prowess of the Crown Heights Affair. Electronics are totally absent from this recording, apart from a series of synth incisions made during breaks in the harmonized chorus. Hand drums and tambourine are played with mechanical precision. Plus, it's a song about dancing, and I think that's something we can all get behind.

Opus Seven was enjoying its fair share of success, playing East Winston haunts like the Dungeon and the Stag, and also touring with the likes of Kool and the Gang, the Commodores, and Confunkshun. But the gas crisis of 1979 changed everything. Like the nation's depleted gas pumps, performance opportunities also dried up. Clubs, suffering a drop in attendance, began hiring DJs for a fraction of what bands were charging. The final straw would occur after a New Year's Eve show in Columbia, South Carolina, when Opus Seven's trailer would jackknife, leaving the members unharmed but strewing their equipment all over the highway. Songs like "Bussle," however, have managed to withstand the test of time, equipment spills and gas shortages be damned. ⊙

–*Jon Kirby*

DO YOU KNOW WHAT
LOU DONALDSON
TRACK WAS SAMPLED
BY BRAND NUBIAN
AND BIGGIE?

WHAT MAJOR SAMPLE
IS FEATURED IN
DR. DRE'S
"THE NEXT EPISODE"?

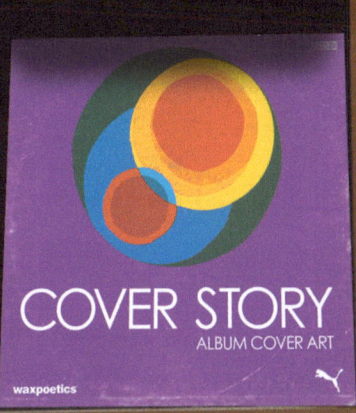

MAIN SOURCE, DE LA, AND
TRIBE ALL SAMPLED A
DONALD BYRD TRACK.

CAN YOU NAME THE
ORIGINAL SOURCE
AND THE SONGS THE
SAMPLE APPEARED IN?

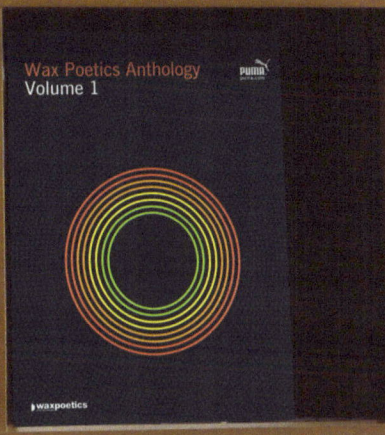

WANT TO KNOW HOW SCHOOLED YOU ARE IN HIP-HOP?

Enter the Droppin' Science trivia contest at www.bluenote.com/droppinscience and prove your skills! You could win cool swag from Blue Note Records and Wax Poetics!

Three (3) winners will be selected from correct contest entries to win the following prizes:

1st Prize: Two (2) Blue Note t-shirts, one (1) *Droppin' Science* CD, two (2) copies of the *Droppin' Science* LP and promo 12", one (1) copy of the new *Wax Poetics Anthology* book, and one (1) two-year subscription to *Wax Poetics Magazine*.

2nd Prize: one (1) *Droppin' Science* CD, two (2) copies of the *Droppin' Science* LP, one (1) copy of the *Wax Poetics Cover Story* book, and one (1) one-year subscription to *Wax Poetics Magazine*.

3rd Prize: one (1) *Droppin' Science* CD, one (1) copy of the *Wax Poetics Cover Story* book, and one (1) one-year subscription to *Wax Poetics Magazine*.

For official contest rules please visit www.bluenote.com/droppinscience/rules.

Blue Note is *Droppin' Science*, bringing it back to the lab of the jazz, funk, and soul chemists who gave the label some of the most influential and groundbreaking music of their time. We've dug deep into the crates to spotlight some of our most treasured works, as we tip our hat to some of the greatest hip-hop artists and producers ever.

WHO GOT DA PROPS? THE FINEST IN JAZZ, HANDS DOWN.

www.bluenote.com
© 2008 Blue Note Records

CORNELL CAMPBELL *Reggae Sun*
AMO RECORDS / CARRERE
1980

One of *Saturday Night Live*'s classic lines—from the "Stand Up and Win" skit—goes: "Who's the ad wizard who came up with that one?" Enter this French-pressed Cornell Campbell LP that shows how neon colors, when handled by a *Miami Vice*–inspired art director in the early '80s, can be a dangerous weapon. So…what happened? In 1976, these ten heavy roots-reggae tracks (including "Gorgon," "Press Along Natty Dread," and some soul covers) by the singer dubbed the "Jamaican Curtis Mayfield" came out on the classic *Gorgon* album, on the Total Sounds label. Everything was fine until its producer, Bunny Lee, never short of a licensing deal, decided to sell the rights of *Gorgon* to Amo Records. This is precisely when graphic murder was committed. The French company apparently wasn't too down with beautiful Jamaican artwork—in the *Gorgon* case, a decently sketched portrait of the singer. The ad wizard came, saw, and damaged: the 1980-issued Amo sleeve then featured this amazing reproduction of a switchblade knife and a different title: *Reggae Sun*. Likewise, half a dozen other Bunny Lee LPs got the same treatment. All called *Reggae Sun*, they rocked an unidentified fluorescent cocktail (for a split Ronnie Davis/Gregory Isaacs—spelled "Isaack"—LP), a marijuana leaf–adorned pack of cigarettes (Barrington Spence's *Tears on My Pillow*), and a few other '80s obsessions. Not to mention a caricature of a Black man on the Clint Eastwood LP—a mind-boggling genius move when you come to learn that these records primarily served as subscription gifts to the teenage female readers of the African edition of *Podium* magazine and *Girls* magazine. On the bright side, the whole *Reggae Sun* series is relatively easy to find at flea markets in France today, as the records' disfigured sleeves save them from the voracious jaws of eBay. For this reason, and this reason only, all hail the ad wizard!

–*Seb Carayol*

Gilles Peterson chooses his favorite Nuyorican sounds from the legendary Fania, Tico, Alegre & Cotique labels.

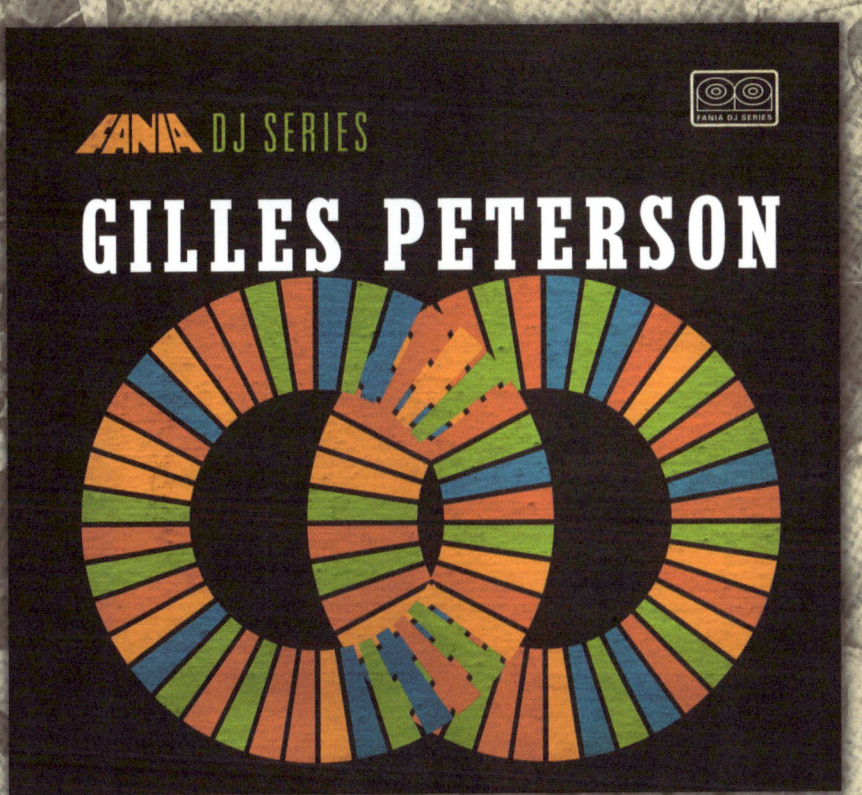

ALSO AVAILABLE

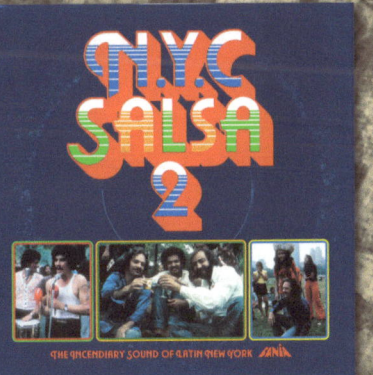

The second in an incredible series digging deep into the vaults of Fania. The original was big, brassy and percussive. Now, we dug a little deeper and reached into the Cotique, Vaya and Tico labels to create NYC 2.

The merging of styles "Cuban and Jazz." Originals on this album still remain impossible to find and are spoken about in hushed tones.

Another set of distinctly El Barrio grooves fit to rock any block party. The sounds of the Spanish Harlem Streets of the 70s.

Rare reissues, new compilations, remixes and more.
Check out all our releases at faniarecords.com

re:Discovery

CASUAL-T "Hands Off"
56 HOPE ROAD
1983

When I used to work in a certain secondhand record store in Manchester, England, there was this Jamaican guy who'd come in and sell us some of the most insane reggae and dub records. This guy would sell 45s for about a pound each (just shy of two bucks), 12-inches for not much more, and would only ever sell things he had spare copies of. I came into work one day, and there was a stack of stuff that had been bought from this guy. Halfway through listening to this pile, there was a boogie record, on the well-known reggae imprint, 56 Hope Road. I'll never forget the feeling of hearing the first few bars of that record. I mean, hearing new boogie records is fairly common, but hearing one like *this* isn't. Maybe it was because I was expecting to hear a crackly roots riddim from this 45 that it had such an effect on me: an overwhelming sense of, "Wow." Or maybe, just maybe, it was because I was playing the "Version" side by mistake, where the vocals only come in on the chorus, and the whole rhythm track, apart from vocals and claps, drops out randomly, dub style. I was so excited that I went home and did my research. The vocal side (which is nowhere near as good, in my opinion) was included on a compilation called *Disc "O" Lypso* a few years back, but that was all I could find. It turns out that Casual-T did in fact do one album, entitled *Prescriptions of Love*, which came out on the Rita Marley/Tuff Gong label, in 1983, but again, only the vocal side features, *not* the version. It also fetches serious money when you can find one for sale. God bless the two-buck-45s guy.

–Ryan Hunn

WONDERWHEEL RECORDINGS
2008 RELEASES

The Pimps of Joytime "Hi Steppin" REMIXES March 2008 Digital Release

Remixes of their debut album "Hi Steppin" plus exclusive new tunes from one of Brooklyn's funkiest & diverse bands of the year!

ZEB "Stop the Earth, I Want to Get Off" REMIXES & REDUBS March 2008 Digital Release

More of that Africa vs Arabia in DUB sound from various remixers around the Globe plus new unreleased songs.

Turntables on the Hudson
10 YEAR ANNIVERSARY BOXSET Summer 2008

10 Years of Music & Dance from one of NYC's longest running parties! The box set will include a CD of some hard to find songs from the first 5 years + new exclusive songs & new DJ mixes from Nickodemus & Mariano + Nappy G on percussion. Also included will be an extensive online photo & flyer exhibit!

Also available on 12" vinyl:

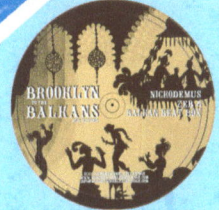

WONDER-16: Nickodemus, ZEB, Balkan Beat Box "Brooklyn to the Balkans & Beyond" 4 track EP

WONDER-17: Nickodemus & Quantic feat Hector 'Tempo' Alomar "Mi Swing es Tropical" ZEB Remix b/w Nickodemus feat Sammy Ayala "Conmigo"

WONDER-18: The Pimps of Joytime "Street Sound" Hi Perspective Remix b/w "Bonita" DJ ORaH Remix

wonderwheelrecordings.com • turntablesonthehudson.com • myspace.com/nickodemusnyc

re:Discovery

MARINI "Africa Must Unite/ Let's Get It On"
KD-LYN RECORDS
1981

"Open your eyes and look closer" is the opening line of the second track on this holy onion of a 12-inch. Sometimes there is treasure buried under the treasure.

Marini, a member of the mid-'70s New York B.W.A.I. Sonatas Steel Orchestra, is the face out front; but she is singing the words of her father, Lynton C. Raphael. The cryptic liner notes tell us that he was inspired by the 1970 Trinidadian Black Power movement, "the now defunct African Mobilization committee of Brooklyn, NY; the teachings of Dr. Yosef ben Jochannan, fondly called D. Ben, noted African historian of Harlem, NY, and the many other leaders." It has the feel of international intrigue as layers peel away to other layers, and the story shifts quickly from one man's words to another's philosophy, and finally to the African struggle.

"Africa must unite by the twenty-first century" is the call to arms that Marini sings repeatedly over the happy calypso of the first track. With its bouncy rhythm and infectious bass line, the song skips along until a squealing synthesizer wakes the sleeping giant that is protecting its deeper secrets. Music is credited to Ibbis, with arrangements provided by George Victory. The name of the band refers to the ibis, a bird of great religious import in ancient Egypt that was often associated with the god Thoth. He was said to have created himself out of the power of language and to have given man the gift of writing. He was also seen as the divine mediator, the one who questioned the souls of the dead as they tried to get to the underworld.

As we peel back the final layer of mystery, George Victory reveals himself to be the shining boogie knight who will take us to heaven. His arrangements borrow heavily from Patrick Adams and Greg Carmichael, as hinted on the title track. But when he gets to take over the show on the synth-heavy "Let's Get It On," the swirling miasma of sexual innuendo and spiritual rebirth find a perfect match with his gruff vocals and the undulating '80s disco beat. ●

–Robbie Busch

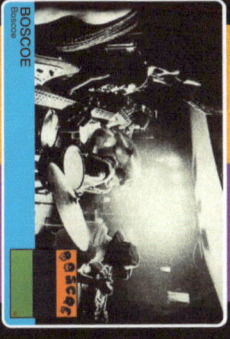

Collect them all!
www.numerogroup.com

re:Discovery

KAREN YOUNG "Hot Shot"
WEST END RECORDS
1978

When Mel Cheren passed away in December 2007, reports of his death understandably referenced the pivotal role he played in the disco and nightlife scene of New York in its heyday of the late '70s and '80s. His label, West End, as well as his roles as financial backer to the Paradise Garage and mentor to DJ Larry Levan, is well known. Cheren also unwittingly provided hip-hop with two primal b-boy classics—a couple of records that were staples of any early jam and whose breaks provided many a current veteran with their introduction to cutting doubles.

One of these was "Sesso Matto," a re-pressing of a 1973 Italian soundtrack whose title track happened to have a good beat (and a chorus a lot like "Soul Makossa"). The other record had Cheren's more direct input, and was West End Records' first bona fide hit.

"Karen Young was a white soul singer from Philadelphia who had once dated Wilson Pickett," writes Cheren in his autobiography. "She was frumpy, knew nothing about makeup and clothes, loved her Quaaludes and was afraid of heights." But Cheren heard something he liked in an unreleased song she'd recorded called "Hot Shot." He decided to release an extended disco mix, which included a long percussion break preceded by a Young vocal riff on the title. It was this bit that reportedly inspired Grandmaster Flash to experiment with back-spinning (in other words, using two copies of a record to run the same phrase in quick succession as a prelude to letting the full break drop).

The song itself, while regarded as a disco classic, may be a little camp for most. But it underscores the lesser-acknowledged symbiotic relationship that dance music had with early hip-hop, and birthed one the most popular early breakbeats. ⊙

–Andrew Mason

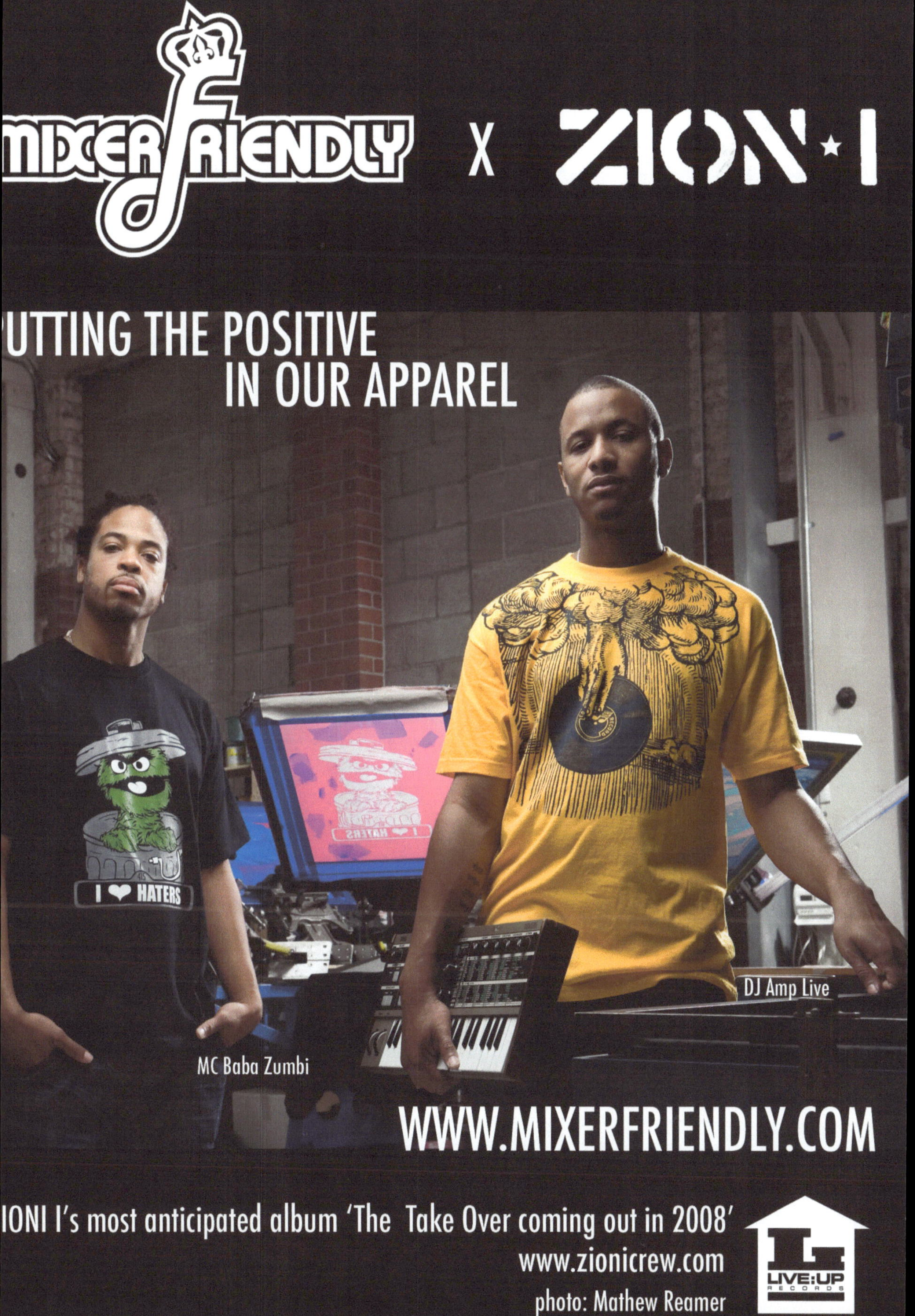

PUTTING THE POSITIVE IN OUR APPAREL

MC Baba Zumbi

DJ Amp Live

WWW.MIXERFRIENDLY.COM

ZIONI I's most anticipated album 'The Take Over coming out in 2008'

www.zionicrew.com

photo: Mathew Reamer

In Memoriam

JOEL DORN
1942–2007

The Masked Announcer Has Left the Auditorium

text
John Kruth

photography
David Gahr

Record producer Joel Dorn, who steered albums by Roberta Flack, Max Roach, Herbie Mann, Les McCann and Eddie Harris, Mose Allison, Rahsaan Roland Kirk, Yusef Lateef, and the Neville Brothers, died of a heart attack on Monday, December 17, in New York. He was sixty-five.

Born in Yeadon, Pennsylvania, on April 7, 1942, Joel grew up listening to Philadelphia radio, obsessed with Ray Charles, the Coasters, the Drifters, and other Atlantic artists. At age fourteen, Dorn sent Nesuhi Ertegun, the head of Atlantic's jazz wing, a critique of their discs with suggestions for sessions he would like to see produced. Joel also said he hoped to work for the label one day.

Dorn's musical career began as a disc jockey in 1961 at Philly's jazz radio station WHAT. "The DJ gig was a great way to get to know all the record companies and get involved in the business, but I had my heart set on producing the entire time," he said in a recent interview. As a producer, Dorn cited Jerry Leiber, Mike Stoller, and Phil Spector as three of his biggest influences.

In 1963, Ertegun gave Dorn his first shot as a record producer, and, with a two-thousand-dollar budget, he signed and recorded flautist Hubert Laws's debut, *The Laws of Jazz*.

Joel relied on his gut instinct when it came to music, telling an interviewer in 1997: "A bell goes off in your stomach when you see or hear something that grabs you." Over the years, that bell rang for everything from jazz to folk to rock, from commercial to eclectic. Dorn signed Bette Midler and produced her debut, *The Divine Miss M*, won two Grammy Awards for Roberta Flack's "The First Time Ever I Saw Your Face," three more for her "Killing Me Softly with His Song," and another for Asleep at the Wheel's cover of Count Basie's "One O'Clock Jump." He was at the helm for sessions with everyone from the Allman Brothers, Donny Hathaway, Mink DeVille, and Don McLean, to jazz bagpiper Rufus Harley, Gary Burton, and Keith Jarrett. Add to that list Gene McDaniels's acid funk opus *Headless Heroes of the Apocalypse* and Les McCann and Eddie Harris's *Swiss Movement* with the soul-jazz smash "Compared to What?" Some of his sonic experiments with Yusef Lateef, like *The Doctor Is In and Out*, contained some of the most cutting-edge music of the '70s. Inspired by Fellini and Magritte, Joel produced music that was surreal, cinematic, and beyond categorization. It wasn't about gold or platinum records or Grammys. It was about risk.

"The guys I brought to Atlantic and produced were all people who'd gotten their initial fame and recognition as jazz musicians, but a lot of time what we did had little to do with jazz. It was more about improvisation. It wasn't the serious, accepted jazz of the moment," Joel told me recently.

Dorn was the tireless champion of the blind multi-instrumentalist Rahsaan Roland Kirk, producing his greatest works, which included *The Inflated Tear*, *Volunteered Slavery*, and *Bright Moments*. After Kirk's death in 1977, Joel was the single person responsible for keeping Rahsaan's music alive.

After leaving Atlantic in 1974, Dorn went on to produce Leon Redbone's debut *On the Track* and the Neville Brothers' 1981 classic *Fiyo on the Bayou*.

In recent years, Joel founded a series of small labels that included Night Records, 32 Jazz, Label M, and most recently Hyena, which has released a series of blues/funk albums by James "Blood" Ulmer, as well as archival tapes of Dr. John, Thelonious Monk, and Joe Williams. Dorn was nominated once again for another Grammy for *The Heavyweight Champion*, a seven-CD box set of John Coltrane's Atlantic recordings.

At the time of his death, Dorn had just finished compiling a five-CD box of classic Atlantic jazz entitled *Homage A Nesuhi*, dedicated to his mentor, Nesuhi Ertegun.

Joel was a great mentor as well—to producers Hal Willner, Michael Cuscuna, and his son Adam (aka Mocean Worker), as well as myself, who he generously allowed to coproduce a couple of Rahsaan Roland Kirk's posthumous discs.

Joel's passing is a great loss to American music and culture. He is survived by his three sons, Michael, Adam, and David, and his wife, Faye Rosen. ◐

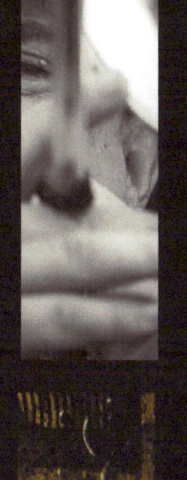

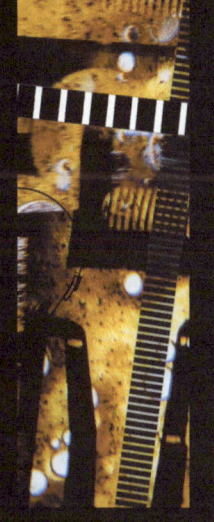

In Memoriam

CARLOS "PATATO" VALDES
1926–2007

The Little Giant

text
Matt Rogers

photography
Martin Cohen

The late, great conguero and bandleader Ray Barretto said it best when introducing a particular gentleman, both mentor and peer, at a Conga Kings concert in New York City a few years ago. As this diminutive "legend, [who's] been preaching our music about as long as the earth was formed," ambled to the stage wearing his signature derby, Barretto expounded with pride. "He's made such an impact in music and left such a beautiful legacy in the world of percussion and improvisation...the little giant, Carlos 'Patato' Valdés." The world of music lost this certified *maestro del ritmo* on December 4, 2007, when conguero Carlos Valdés, better known simply by his nickname, Patato, joined that ever-growing master class in the sky. He was eighty-one.

Generally acknowledged as the first conguero to tune his conga drums, Valdés had an illustriously long and star-studded career, one which began in Cuba, then, via his electric landmark style in the clubs and studios of New York City, took him all around the world, making stops on television and the silver screen, and, in the process, placing him in the pantheon of conga greats like Chano, Mongo, Candido, Aguabella, Sabu, and Barretto.

Born November 4, 1926, in Havana, Cuba, to a musical family (true, which family in Cuba isn't), Patato became proficient on several instruments, including his father's—the tres. In his teens, however, he focused on the congas and soon played for rumbas and orchestras in the streets and on TV, where he liked to showcase his ability to play *and* dance on top of his drums without missing a beat. In the early '50s, when mambo was the rage, Patato visited NYC and was impressed with the Latin jazz scene in which many of his Cuban peers had helped forge; so much so, the conguero emigrated to the Big Apple with the help of his longtime friend Mongo Santamaria, who also landed him a spot with his at-the-time gig, the Tito Puente Orchestra. Once established as a part of one of the city's top dance bands, it wasn't long before Patato's hands made their imprint on the recorded world of jazz (Latin and otherwise).

In '55, the often mischievous conguero found himself in the company of jazz heavyweights Horace Silver, Art Blakey, Oscar Pettiford, and Kenny Dorham for the latter's sophomore full-length, *Afro-Cuban* for Blue Note. If he was intimidated, you'd never know it, his playing in the forefront for much of the album. From here, his recording career as sideman was all-systems-go, as he had a knack to help mold seminal albums by music's finest, a who's who list including Quincy Jones, Max Roach, Machito, Cal Tjader, Grant Green, Dizzy, Elvin Jones, Herbie Mann, Willie Bobo, and Tito Puente. "Of all the conguero masters," says Johnny Griggs, himself a conguero who would go on to break many a funky beat for James Brown and Pucho, "Patato was the most tuneful and melodic—and intense!"

In addition to Puente, Patato did long stints fortifying the live percussion sections of folks like Machito and Herbie Mann, and, after years of lending his studio handiwork to others, Patato finally landed a date of his own in '68 with the tall and lanky singer Eugene "Totico" Arango. The resultant masterwork, *Patato & Totico* on Verve (with its classic *Mutt and Jeff*-like cover), is considered a perfect melding of rumba and jazz, enlisting Cuban greats Arsenio Rodriguez and bassist Cachao. Despite the album's acclaim, however, Patato would only record a few more albums as bandleader throughout the remainder of his career, though he would go on to develop his own popular series of tunable congas.

In 2001, Patato began touring and recording with the Conga Kings, a group that also consisted of congueros Candido Camero and Giovanni Hidalgo, thus providing a bookend to a life that influenced several generations of percussionists. As Barretto, who would often play with the Conga Kings in NYC, once said, "Size doesn't tell the story of his gigantic talent." ⊙

In Memoriam

PIMP C
1973–2007

Pimp C Is Free

text
Jon Kirby

photography
Pam Francis/Getty Images

Chad "Pimp C" Butler was born December 29, 1973, in Port Arthur, Texas. This small coastal town, the birthplace of musical pioneers Janis Joplin and DJ Premier, would eventually give birth to one of the most influential rap groups in history, the Underground Kingz, comprised of Pimp C and Bernard "Bun B" Freeman.

UGK would release their first cassette, *The Southern Way*, before their sixteenth birthdays. Butler, whose father played trumpet professionally with soul singer Solomon Burke, handled the bulk of production, while Freeman handled vocal duties. Despite living nearly one hundred miles from the hip-hop hotbed of Houston, UGK's early demos made a major impression on executives at Jive Records, who signed the duo to a five-album deal in 1992. The group cut a series of well-received records before releasing 1996's *Ridin' Dirty*, considered by many to be a pivotal album for Southern hip-hop as well as a victory for the mainstream acceptance of "country rap." The motifs on this album were universal, yet quintessentially Southern. Rural poverty, car culture, and race relations were approached from the unique perspective of this gifted team of lyricists.

UGK would reach another mile marker in 2000 when Jay-Z invited Butler and Freeman to appear on the Timbaland-produced single "Big Pimpin'." Months later, Three 6 Mafia would feature UGK on "Sippin' on Some Syrup," the first of many odes to the Texas intoxicant, named after the drink's active ingredient, cough syrup. Both hits would win them and their respective collaborators mainstream acclaim in both Northern and Southern hip-hop markets.

But just as momentum was building for UGK, Butler would be incarcerated due to parole violations related to a previous assault charge. While serving an eight-year prison sentence, Freeman would front a "Free Pimp C" campaign that would find supporters from all corners of hip-hop music. T-shirts could be seen and shout-outs heard over the following years, as rappers would pay homage to UGK's stifled potential.

In 2005, Butler would be released from jail after serving only half of his original sentence. After visiting briefly with his wife and children, Butler hit the studio to cut a remake of UGK's "Front and Back" with T.I., as well as a remix of Bun B's solo single, "Get Throwed."

"I put together over 2,500 songs in jail," Butler told *Rolling Stone* upon his release. "I did them all on loose-leaf paper. When I'd get ten songs, I'd mail them home so that they wouldn't get lost in the sauce. They're still all in the envelopes—I got a shopping bag full of rhymes."

Many of these rhymes would find a home on UGK's long-awaited 2006 release, *UGK*, an astounding thirty-one-song offering, featuring a rap spectrum of cameos from Talib Kweli to Lil Jon, Marley Marl to Too Short, who Butler was slated to record an album with. *UGK* debuted at number one on the *Billboard* charts and has since achieved gold status.

But just as the Texas team was poised for greatness, the greatest of misfortunes occurred. Three days after performing alongside Too Short at Hollywood's House of Blues, Butler was found dead in his hotel room. He passed in his sleep due to natural causes. Few took the news harder than Freeman, who had already flown the UGK flag through numerous trials and tribulation. However, when an emotional Freeman appeared on Houston's KBXX just days after the tragedy, his mood was optimistic.

"I said everything I needed to say to Pimp. I have no regrets about anything. I know that the last time I saw him, I hugged him, and I told him I loved him, which was what I did every time I saw him. 'Cause you never know how things in life is going to work out—and that is one regret I won't have." ⊙

Available Now
* Brand Nubian - Times Running Out
* Rob-O - Rhyme Pro
* Dooley-O - Basement Tapes

Upcoming Releases 2008
* **Grand Puba w/Lord Finesse**
* **Cold Heat**
  Jak Danielz & Johnny Walker
  FEAT Craig G, Sadat-X, Buckshot
  PRODUCTION BY Lord Finesse, Psycho LES, & JS-1
* **Absynth OST**
  FEAT Thurston Moore, MV + EE, Sun City Girls
* **Blacastan**
* **GTV Complete Series**

Sound of Dissent Rare Vinyl Online Store
Records   Weekly Podcasts - Graffiti Database
www.soundofdissent.com

SOD Party Last Wednesday of Every Month
PALOMA 60 Greenpoint Ave. Brooklyn

In Memoriam

OSCAR PETERSON
1925–2007

From Scott Joplin
Till the Day After Tomorrow

text
John Kruth

photography
Michael Ochs Archives/Getty Images

Born August 15, 1925, Oscar Emmanuel Peterson grew up in the poor, mostly Black neighborhood of Montreal's Little Burgundy. By age five, he began playing piano and trumpet but dropped the horn two years later after a long, difficult bout with tuberculosis. Although initially trained in classical music, Peterson loved the stride style of James P. Johnson and would earn the nickname the "Brown Bomber of Boogie-Woogie."

Oscar's technical mastery was unparalleled, second only to the blind genius Art Tatum, whose frenetic "Tiger Rag" caused Oscar crying fits and to quit the piano for two months. Peterson then became the sole Black member of Johnny Holmes's Orchestra, touring Canada and the U.S., where he learned first hand the bitter realities of segregation.

In 1947, impresario Norman Granz heard Peterson performing live on the radio in Montreal and grabbed a cab over to meet him. After convincing Oscar to drop the boogie and focus more on standards, he became a mainstay of Granz's Jazz at the Philharmonic series. Two years later, Oscar made his stunning debut at Carnegie Hall. By 1950, he'd won the first of many *Down Beat* polls for best jazz pianist. From 1953 to 1958, the Oscar Peterson Trio, with guitarist Herb Ellis and bassist Ray Brown, was truly one of the great groups of jazz.

Composer/multi-instrumentalist David Amram, who first met Oscar in Paris in 1955, regaled him as a "world-class virtuoso, hardworking, serious, an extraordinarily accomplished musician, who personified the spirit of jazz. Along with his musical brilliance and technical wizardry, he had the true egalitarian spirit, because, when he was done working, he'd go out and play jam sessions and encourage others to play. Coming from Canada, I think he had to work that much harder. He was one of the people like Django Reinhardt that showed you that you could be from anywhere and still make a contribution to jazz. Like a great scholar, he not only knew the history of the music but was able to play it, from Scott Joplin till the day after tomorrow."

While Duke Ellington and Count Basie praised Oscar's prowess, and his fingers could fly over the keyboard in displays of dazzling technical virtuosity, many critics complained that Peterson's playing lacked soul. Les McCann begs to differ: "I never heard a record that had so much emotion before as his version of 'Tenderly.' You could actually feel what was goin' on. I knew if I could ever accomplish something like that, I'd be happy. It might take people a little while to realize just how great he really was, for the truth to get out."

Peterson was one of the most prolific artists in jazz, with an enormous discography boasting over two hundred albums that earned him eight Grammy Awards. Throughout his life, he maintained a hectic touring schedule, playing clubs and festivals across North America, Europe, and Japan, while releasing up to four or five records a year, mostly on the Verve and Pablo labels. When not performing solo or with his trio, Oscar accompanied many of the music's greatest singers, including Louis Armstrong, Nat King Cole, and Ella Fitzgerald, as well as cutting-edge improvisers like Charlie Parker, Dizzy Gillespie, and Roy Eldridge. Two of his most surprising collaborations included duets with keyboardists Herbie Hancock and Keith Emerson.

In 1993, Oscar suffered a debilitating stroke that limited the use of his left hand, yet he still continued to record and perform occasionally. Peterson died on December 23 of kidney failure at home in Mississauga, Ontario, outside Toronto. He was eighty-two. ○

RELEASE DATE: FEBRUARY 12, 2008

RELEASE DATE: FEBRUARY 19, 2008

CHRIS JOSS
"Joss Fuses together House, psychedelic synths, funk and bossa nova with moments of energy surge and acid jazz textures."
— IDJ magazine

URSULA 1000
"A collection of exclusive remixes culled from The album "Hear Comes Tomorrow" with remixes by Fort Knox Five, J-Star, Skeewiff and Ladytron."

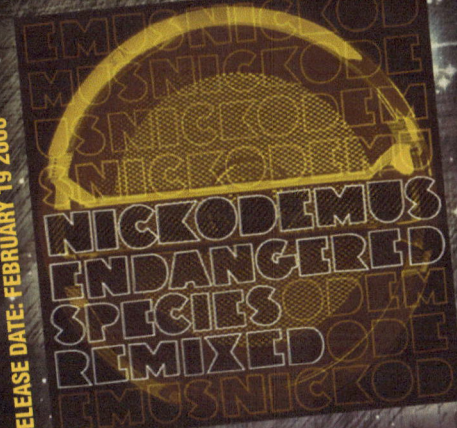

RELEASE DATE: FEBRUARY 19 2008

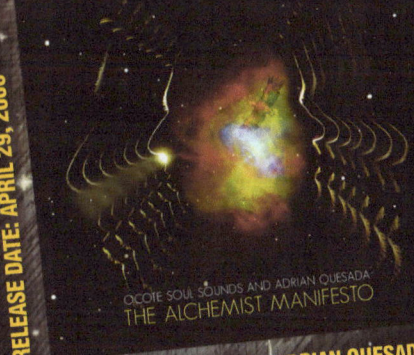

RELEASE DATE: APRIL 29, 2008

NICKODEMUS
"Amazing mix of hip hop, house, afrobeat, klezmer, afrocubano and just about everything else you can think of chopped in a blender and made refreshing. This album includes a remix of "Mi Swing es Tropical", the track featured in the Itunes' commercial."

OCOTE SOUL SOUND AND ADRIAN QUESADA
"A whirlpool of psychedelic Afro-beat that's tethered by a Latin sound."
— Wax Poetics

RELEASE DATE: MAY 2008

2008 NEW RELEASES

eslmusic.com

NATALIA CLAVIER
"Natalia is the languid and haughty voice of Federico's Aubele's Panamericana"
— Mojo Magazine

TOM TERRELL
1950–2007

Lost in Music

text
Richard Torres

photo essay
Tom Terrell

Calling my friend Tom Terrell a renaissance man is like calling Frank Sinatra a singer or Miles Davis a trumpeter. Yeah, the description's accurate, but it doesn't capture the encompassing artistry of these men in either their professions or how they lived their lives. See, in actuality, Terrell—a self-described "native New Jersey guy" who was born on July 16, 1950, and died of bone and prostate cancer in Washington, D.C., on November 29, 2007—was much closer to the jet-set-age model of the modern man. A professional multihyphenate, Terrell was a superlative writer and photographer whose work appeared in many publications like *Vibe*, *Global Rhythm*, and *The Village Voice*, as well as this magazine. He'd contributed essays to several books, including *The Breaks* and *The Vibe History of Hip Hop*. A Howard University graduate, Terrell made a name for himself during the '80s as *the* influential radio personality "Lil Tommy Tee" for WHFS-FM and as a club DJ for the famed 9:30 Club in the District. What Terrell brought to *all* these gigs was a voluminous knowledge of every music genre. He'd fearlessly, seamlessly mix reggae with country, punk with Afropop, soul with metal, rap with house, and salsa with zouk. In other words, he brought musical democracy to the nation's capital.

Yet, when I met him at a party for the film *The Hot Spot* in 1990, he'd just traded in his notoriety to take a promotions gig for Mango/Antilles Records in New York City. Quick recap of said meeting: we chatted; he told me that the flick's soundtrack had John Lee Hooker playing with Miles, saw the excitement in my eyes over said info, and gave me his last promo CD on the spot. For true musicologists and promosexuals, this is the stuff that beautiful friendships are instantly made of. Years later, when I asked him why he would give up such exalted status to start all over in the Big Apple, he quickly, decisively replied: "Rich, what good is life without risk?"

It was that adventurous spirit that I loved about Tom Terrell. He was down to see any new band, exhibit, or performance space. It was all part of the artistic continuum. If I had a "plus one"—industry-speak for an extra concert ticket—he was ready to check it out. And vice versa. Over the years, it seemed we caught everyone from Prince to Taj Mahal, from Ricky Martin to Beth Orton, from his beloved aunt Shirley Horn to Eddie Palmieri, and any Marsalis with an instrument. During each show, I'd turn to look at Terrell. He'd have his eyes tightly closed and his head swaying to the beat, absorbing all and filing it away in his encyclopedic mind. Later, when we did our concert recap, not only could he recall the evening's set in order but also the soloists and what they played.

That phenomenal memory plus his emotional connection to music are what elevated Tom Terrell over fellow critics. At a show, while other scribes sat on their hands and stared at the performers onstage, he reacted. I recall during a thrilling passage at an Ornette Coleman concert at Lincoln Center, he nudged me in the ribs and pointed out the critics sitting across the aisle from us. While the raucous crowd shouted out their exhortations, the critical cognoscenti did their usual Easter Island statue impersonation. "Man," said Terrell, "if you can't *feel* the music, why bother showing up?"

And, after he left a publicist job at Verve Records in 1996, Terrell devoted himself to getting that feeling across in his writing and photography. In regards to the latter, Terrell was Zelig with a telephoto lens. Affectionately dubbed "Shutter" by his Howard classmates, he had seen and snapped every major act either coming up or in their glory. The result was an impressive library that documented acts like James Brown and Run-DMC at their most exciting. In the midst of the CD reissue boom, many labels used his invaluable photos to augment their packaging.

Even more impressive were his liner notes for these reissues. Terrell took these assignments very seriously and, working within tight editorial constraints, used his idiosyncratic neo-hipster voice to create witty conversational gems packed with historical recaps, musical insights, and sly humor for diverse acts like Ellen McIlwaine, Roy Ayers, Mongo Santamaria, Eric B. and Rakim, Steel Pulse, and the Gap Band. A raconteur, Terrell was also the best talk-show guest the *Late Show* never had. When asked what the original Woodstock was like, he immediately responded: "Lots of sex, lots of drugs, and, like anyone who was too busy doing the first two, I had to see the movie to find out about the rock and roll."

A couple of years ago, daunted by New York's rising rents, Terrell returned to D.C. Along with his usual writings, he was contributing to National Public Radio and programming the XM satellite radio station World Zone when he was diagnosed with cancer. In support of Terrell, a plethora of musicians—Coati Mundi, Vernon Reid, and Chuck Brown among them—whom he'd championed throughout the years, performed at benefits for him in both New York and Washington in late 2006 and early 2007. Even as the insidious disease wreaked havoc on his body, the memory of love shown towards him at those shows, he told me just weeks before he passed, always lifted his spirit. His major regret, he continued, was not finishing a memoir he'd provocatively entitled *Bitches, Blips & Bops: 40 Years Lost in Music*. But, in a sense, he had. Like the artists he admired and documented, he had bared himself in every word he wrote, in every picture he took, in every interview he conducted, in every story he told, in every segue he made. Tom Terrell was lost in music and made us—myself, in particular—grateful to be part of the journey.

Tom Terrell in Paris, circa 1973
photo courtesy of Jeff The Purple

Kurtis Blow: 9:30 Club, Washington, D.C. 1981
(Check Russell Simmons in front row)

HOWLIN' WOLF · HOWARD UNIVERSITY · NOV. 1970

BOB MARLEY · SURVIVAL TOUR PARTY · WASH., D.C. 1979

Bill Summers · Headhunters

Ras Michael. "Morning Meditation". Nov. 1981

THE 2008 xB.

Vehicle shown is a special project car, modified with non-Genuine Scion parts and accessories. Modification with these non-Genuine Scion parts or accessories will void the Scion warranty, may negatively impact vehicle performance & safety, and may not be street legal. © 2007 Scion is a marque of Toyota Motor Sales, USA, Inc.

Border Crossing
Brownout traffics in Tejano funk

text
Kristofer Rios

photography
David Gilder

Since 2003, the eight-piece funk band Brownout has been rocking b-boy jams and packing live-music venues with fast-paced funk covers. While Brownout may be a relatively new band on the block, the group's front men, Adrian Quesada, Beto Martinez, Greg Gonzales, and Johnny Lopez, have been redefining Latin music for years with their orchestra, Grupo Fantasma. The orchestra has dominated music festivals and won countless awards with their funky blend of cumbias, salsa, and merengue. As Brownout, they are looking to rediscover their funkier beginnings.

Quesada, Martinez, Gonzales, and Lopez started their musical journey as a high school funk-rock garage band in the booming border town of Laredo, Texas. Initially, their band was a teenage musical revolt against their parents' beloved Mexican cumbias and Tejano music. But their immersion into the worlds of Sly Stone, James Brown, and Mandrill would verse them in soulful drum breaks, deep-in-the-pocket guitar riffs, and groovy bass lines, providing the foundation for later incarnations of the band. As the four grew older, they migrated out of the garage, four hours north into Austin's thriving music scene. Inspired by their parents' music and their Latino heritage, they formed Grupo Fantasma to explore the cumbia rhythms they rejected as teenagers.

Still searching for the perfect vessel through which to channel their musical inspirations and contain their endless creative energy, Brownout has become the team's breakbeat-kicking, horn-line-slinging, funkdafied *luchador* alter ego. The band's debut album, *Homenaje*, or "Homage," is a tribute to the group's musical gods: an eclectic pantheon including Latin-rock legends Carlos Santana, Chepito Areas, and Malo; trombonist Fred Wesley; Southern Texas Tejano musicians Little Joe and Ruben Ramos; and Afrobeat king Fela Kuti, to name a few. The result is a distinct, homegrown brew of Afro-Latin funkiness filled with backbeat-heavy drum lines, vamped up montunos, fluent guitar solos, and spontaneous horn arrangements. With *Homenaje*, Brownout has extracted all the best parts of their influences—each track hauntingly familiar, yet distinct in its own style. "Brown Wind and Fire," the album's opening track, shows off the group's more soulful roots; its rolling bass line sets a cool pace, while its eerie guitar—a nod to Santana—dances around the groove. Other tracks—"Homenaje," "Con El Brownout No Se Juega," and the Manu Dibango cover of "African Battle"—drive the album and manifest the group's funky origins.

The Laredo four can be seen these days closing the generational gap, jamming with JB alumnus Maceo Parker, P-Funk arranger Greg Boyer, and Prince at his royal court in Las Vegas. In the tradition of South Texas border rockers, Brownout has elegantly bridged their multiple musical universes. ⊙

VAMPISOUL

MARIE QUEENIE LYONS
'Soul Fever'
LP & CD
vampi 096

EDDIE BO
'In The Pocket with...'
2Lp & CD
vampi 095

Great female soul album -- reissue of the one and only album cut by Marie Queenie Lyons, for legendary Deluxe label. Very well known for her sought after soulful funky 45s! (see Fever / Your Key don't fit... available on the Vampisoul CRASH OF THUNDER). The entire album is as solid as her 45s – a total classic that will blow minds to the followers of such Soul-divas as Erma Franklin, Barbara Acklin, Marva Whitney, etc… --- AS GOOD AS YOU can imagine.

Awesome compilation of New Orleans hot tracks by the great Mr. Eddie Bo. Well known from his massive hits 'Check Mr. Popeye' and 'Hook & Sling', Eddie Bo have loads of other great songs on this double Lp or digipack format, most of which never got reissued. Here's the musical story of one of the most innovative and unknown composers of the last fifty years.

QUINTEPLUS
'S / T'
2vinyl & CD
vampi 094

RUBEN LOPEZ FURST
'Jazz Argentino en La Universidad'
2vinyl & CD
vampi 093

Founded after the "New Jazz Collective" movement in Argentina in the late 60's. An experiment with Folk genres in a Jazz key, and the exploration of African rythms, as a bridge between both musical worlds. This set contains the only studio album (1972) and a a great bonus: a complete live at a gig from the same year, unreleased until now !

Argentinean Jazz from the 1960s! This two album pack demonstrate the delicate blend of Swing and Moods à la Bill Evans that characterized the Argentinean pianist brilliant playing. Two original records in this pack: "Jazz en la Universidad " (1966), and "Jazz Argentino" (1967). As good wine, this music has improved with time.

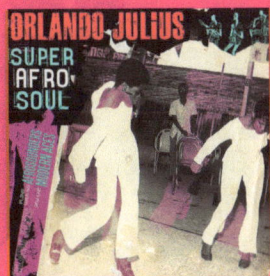

ORLANDO JULIUS
'Super Afro Soul'
3vinyl & 2CD
vampi 091

TONY ALLEN
'Afro Disco Beat'
3vinyl & 2CD
vampi 090

www.vampisoul.com

Distributed by Light in the attic

Crate Moments in History

Blue Note digs golden-era hip-hop

text
Matt Rogers

photography
Michael Ochs Archives/Getty Images

It's rough gettin' old, son. Your internal cogs—physical, mental—once smooth and obedient, start to hem 'n' haw with cantankerous vigor. Ohhh, to be a twenty-something mug all over again when love and acid jazz was in the air, and your tired-ass stories didn't yet play like a pockmarked 7-inch. Well, maybe they skipped then as well but hell if I can remember. What I do recall, though, is rap being hella fresh (I'm crusty now, I'm tellin' ya), a golden age when ol' man Bush was still mannin' this nation's ones and twos, and hip-hop producers were finally lettin' the Godfather of Soul take a nap. And while JB rested, they got *jazzy*.

Record companies like Fantasy, Verve, and, especially, Blue Note smelled gold in them thar forgotten hills and began compiling and reissuing—most notably via their *Blue Break Beats* and *Rare Grooves* series—the now (as in "then") hip sample-fodder that many jazz critics had originally decried as unworthy pop back in the day. The same music that jazz canonizers Kenny (sorta dope) Burns and Wynton Marsalis would still try to forget as Y2K and MP3s kick-started a new millennium.

Well, Blue Note's still redecorating its catalog, this time as *Droppin' Science: Greatest Samples From the Blue Note Lab*, a thirteen-cut collection of originals spanning the years '66–'75. This booty was bit into again and again in the early '90s by such rap royalty as the Beastie Boys, A Tribe Called Quest, De La Soul, Digable Planets, Gang Starr, and many others. This collection is for those in need of a late pass or who were simply too young to snatch up the first reissue go-around. In short, for the kidz. These soul/funk/jazz classics—propelled by such rare-groove luminaries as Lou Donaldson, Donald Byrd, Ronnie Foster, Grant Green, David Axelrod, Idris Muhammad—though retreaded many a time over the years, still sound fresh.

One listen will refresh your memory as to why hip-hop heads gravitated to these LPs in the first place: for the same reason folks plucked these records when they originally came out a generation earlier, critics be damned: the fatback grease of the groove. Call it soul jazz, funk jazz, acid jazz, fusion. Whatever. A generational dialogue was sparked, particularly when folks like Guru actually opened a phone book and hooked some of these "old-timers" up via his *Jazzmatazz*-mobile, shining the spotlight and resuscitating careers. And Blue Note's Us3, who'd smashed the charts with their Herbie Hancock–rooted "Cantaloop," tapped organist Lonnie Smith to collaborate as well. "I was supposed to rerecord [1969's] 'Move Your Hand' with them—went over to England and found out they'd just broke up," says Dr. Smith, still going strong today, and whose tasty 1970 cover of "Spinning Wheel" is included here. "It was gonna be good too, 'cause you know this music we did so long ago was real; it talked to the people, and it made them *move*."

Still does. Lots of thick Hammond organ (thank you, Smith, Foster, McDuff, Creque) is always welcome. As is Count Basie veteran vocalist Joe Williams who—with the help of the Thad Jones–Mel Lewis Orchestra—*crushes* "Get Out of My Life Woman," reminding us once again swing and funk are indeed kissing cousins.

Brass Reconstruction

New Orleans's Hot 8 are second-line saviors

text
Andrew Mason

photography
Michelle L. Elmore

The Hot 8 Brass Band is a juggernaut of sweat, breath, metal, and drums, a powerhouse that lets nothing get in its way. The New Orleans group has overcome unfathomable circumstances, including the violent deaths of three members. But perhaps their greatest challenge came in the aftermath of Katrina, when the band, like most of the residents of their hometown, had scattered.

They managed to regroup in nearby Baton Rouge and set about borrowing instruments. They had a purpose. "We wanted to play," remembers Bennie Pete, the band's mountainous tuba player and leader. "Like, let's go play at some of the shelters for the evacuees."

He continues: "It was amazing, man. We showed up, and the military was there with their guns. People were just stressing. They didn't know we was coming. We just showed up and started striking up the music, and they couldn't believe it. People were like, 'That's a band! That's a band!' A lot of the military police, a lot of the people who came from different states to help out, they all was amazed. You could see it on they face, because they just was here watching these people sad, crying, worrying about where the rest of their family was at. And then this band, a group of guys hop out with instruments [and] go to playing, and everybody just come run out and go to dancing and rejoicing, and having a good time. That made people feel like everything was all right for that little bit of time."

The Hot 8 came together about a dozen years ago, formed from the remnants of two dissolving groups. "Half of us were from the Lower Ninth Ward, which is downtown, and half of us was from uptown, which is the Third Ward," says Pete. "We had the best of both worlds." The group's true antecedents, however, stretch back to the late 1800s. Raymond Williams, trumpeter with the Hot 8, explains, "The [brass band] tradition goes back all the way to Buddy Bolden, who was the first known trumpet player in New Orleans." One hundred years later, the Hot 8's lineup is not much different from the bands of Bolden's era: two trumpets, one tenor sax, and two trombones, with a rhythm section of a bass drum, hi-hat, and snare.

But it's a safe bet that Bolden's repertoire never included songs like "Atomic Dog" or "Sexual Healing," crowd-igniting Hot 8 standards. Trumpeter Shamarr Allen names Leroy Johnson and the Hurricane Brass Band, and later the Dirty Dozen Brass Band, as the first to incorporate contemporary R&B in their shows, but says bands also have to be able to touch on the traditional classics: "Not just reach back, but reach back and make sense. If you don't, you not a real New Orleans brass band."

The Hot 8 are a definitive New Orleans brass band. Dinerral Shavers, the band's snare drummer, killed in a senseless shooting a year after Katrina, was interviewed on CNN shortly after the hurricane: "We're no different from them. We lost everything too. But we have something that everybody don't have. And it's our music. And we're using the music to the best of our ability to show our appreciation and show that New Orleans don't die." ⊙

The Hot 8 Brass Band's *Rock With the Hot 8* is available on Tru–Thoughts Records and through their website, hot8brassband.com.

DELICIOUS VINYL
20 YEARS FRESH est. 1987

NEW RELEASES

MR. VEGAS
HOT IT UP

JAY DEE
THE DELICIOUS VINYL YEARS

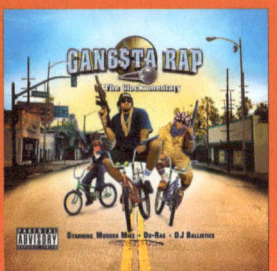
GANGSTA RAP
THE GLOCKUMENTARY

AARON LACRATE & DEBONAIR SAMIR
GUTTER RMXS

STAFF FAVORITES

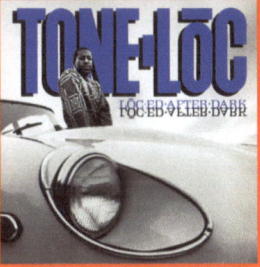
TONE-LOC
LOC'D AFTER DARK

THE PHARCYDE
LABCABINCALIFORNIA

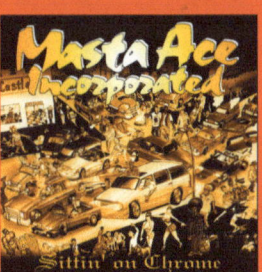
MASTA ACE
SITTIN' ON CHROME

THE BRAND NEW HEAVIES
HEAVY RHYME EXPERIENCE

FATLIP
THE LONELIEST PUNK

THE BRAND NEW HEAVIES
TRUNK FUNK

THE PHARCYDE
BIZZARE RIDE II

MASTA ACE
SLAUGHTAHOUSE

FRESH REMIXES COMING IN MAY '08

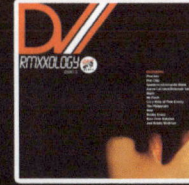

DELICIOUSVINYL.COM
© 2008 Delicious Vinyl, LLC.
6607 Sunset Blvd. Los Angeles, CA 90028

THIS IS IT

Camp Lo wants a piece of the action

text
Jon Kirby

photo courtesy of
Sonny Cheeba

"Today we're going to make the record that's going to change your life," professes Ski Beatz from the back porch of his North Carolina studio. Although Camp Lo's longtime producer is in hit mode, Geechi Suede seems to need a little convincing. Ski is unrelenting in his playful hazing: "Why you lookin' at the ground, B? We're about to win! Yo, we gonna win or what?" As Ski hurls motivational snowballs across the basement-level embankment, Suede paces, shuffling autumn leaves into the yard with his unlaced Timberlands.

"Today," insists Ski. "We're winning today. So all this pain you been going through is for nothing. All this worrying and shit? You're just driving yourself crazy—for nothing. 'Cause you're a star. You been a star, kid. I'm feeling good today; don't make me feel like this."

Ski is like a seasoned boxing trainer. He knows how to critique his contenders with the perfect combination of criticism and encouragement. He's trained victorious heavyweights like Jay-Z, Fat Joe, and even tempered a young Camp Lo for their seamless debut, 1997's *Uptown Saturday Night*. The members of the group were just teenagers at the time of its release, considered in most circles to be a hip-hop classic. It combined the cinematic soul of '70s blaxploitation films with the rich slang of hip-hop's Bronx birthplace. Although *Uptown Saturday Night* featured coffee-shop cameos by De La Soul's Trugoy the Dove and Digable Planets' Butterfly, the bulk of the vocal delivery was executed by marquee MCs Geechi Suede and Sonny Cheeba. Their flows were a patchwork quilt of *Soul Train* and *Rap Attack*. The group quickly rattled off single after single, with the high-budget videos to back them up. "Coolie High" was quickly followed with the anthemic "Luchini aka This Is It," which was countered by "Black Nostaljack aka Come On."

Unfortunately, a follow-up album eluded them for five years. In 2002, the group released *Let's Do It Again*, which, in short, did not exactly do it again. Another five years later, the group has returned to Ski's studio to see if lightning can be enticed to strike in the same place twice.

A major label is nibbling at the Lo line, and, though Camp Lo has not taken any time off since *Let's Do It Again*, the group wants to ensure that they have an action-packed offering to put on the table. Sonny Cheeba has taken a Greyhound bus from Charlotte, and Suede has hitched a ride from Durham with producer and Lo collaborator Stephen Levitin, who has won several regional and national beat battles as the "Apple Juice Kid."

Ski has just returned from a cross-country run with his newest protégé, Pittsburgh Slim, who just signed a half-million dollar deal with Def Jam. Slim is a brash, young White kid from Pennsylvania who just months ago was waiting tables in midtown Manhattan. Slim's first single, "Girls Kiss Girls," is an instant club classic that's been causing coed experimentation on dance floors nationwide. Ski has tasted fresh success and knows that the next Camp Lo hit could be right around the corner. "They should have been had a major deal," insists Ski. "They should have been larger than the Fugees—all these guys, because they're so original, and there's just no original music going on right now." Ski, if anyone, can see where Camp Lo stands in relation to the remainder of the hip-hop universe. "When they came out, they were just so ahead of their time. The time still hasn't caught up with them, if you ask me, because they're still somewhere else."

This is a point that most could agree on. Behind the scenes, the two often prefer the shadows to the limelight. When they converse, it's in a strange Creole of urban banter and twin-speak, a dialect only the two of them seem to fully comprehend. Cheeba and Suede have always dressed, talked, and rapped differently. It is this same quality—this intentional dissonance—that has made Camp Lo hard to market. Esoteric, yet accessible. Classic, yet still contemporary. Out of the gate, the duo shot to the top, only to embark shortly thereafter on a slow, complicated descent into near obscurity. Cameos on records like Aesop Rock's *Bazooka Tooth* and the Lifesavas' *Gutterfly* have kept Camp Lo in indie rotation, but still they trudge on, looking for a record to call their own.

At the turn of the century when Arista Records copped and subsequently dropped the entire Profile catalog, Camp Lo was sent into a downward spiral, becoming nearly mummified in red tape and entombed in label politics. In the five years since Dymond Crook Records released the group's equally suspect second album, the group has been looking for a new home for their new music. After dropping the

> "DON'T OVERANALYZE SHIT—SOMETIMES YOU CAN HOLD YOURSELF BACK FROM GREATNESS."

desert-island single "Gotcha" in 2005, Talib Kweli's Blacksmith Records showed serious interest, but Camp Lo was still contractually bound to shady investors. Finally, Camp Lo is in the clear to produce their third album, tentatively entitled *A Piece of the Action*.

"*A Piece of the Action* got to sound like a piece of the action, know what I'm saying?" says Cheeba from a leather office chair inside the control room. While Cheeba sits at the console, snooping through beats, Ski and Juice are in the adjoining parlor searching for samples. Every time the needle drops, Ski identifies the artists who've used each particular phrase. "Kanye, Jean Grae, Paul Wall." Entire sides of potential platters are exhausted by hip-hop's plagiaristic past. "See, that's why I'm trying to sample stuff that came out last week," jokes Juice, "in Europe."

As far as preparing lyrics, Suede and Cheeba only begin charting out their verbal routes once the beat is completed. "You can't really lay with a song *or* a lyric longer than that first day," states Cheeba, as he awaits the first batch of fresh instrumentals. "We usually finish a joint the same day. If you don't finish it, and the hook ain't there? Nah, it's got to be a complete song for you to feel it all the way out."

Suede's writing style is cerebral to say the least. "Everyone thinks Jay was the first one to not write lyrics," states Ski. "But that's always been Suede. He just always comes in and will look at you like this," motioning to press record. "Next thing you know, he's written a whole rhyme in his head."

It was this very formula that rendered Lo's first international single, "Luchini," a song that holds no shortage of sentimental value for the group, even ten years later.

"I remember just going into the crate, droppin' the needle, and hearing them horns," remembers Ski, still excited from his legendary interpretation of Dynasty's "Adventures in the Land of Music." "I chopped it up that day and called Lo and said, 'Yo, you got to come and hear this beat!'" Within hours, Cheeba and Suede had written their verses, Ski had contributed a hook, and the tapes were sent to Profile, who insisted that "Luchini" become the follow-up single to "Coolie High."

But in a parallel universe, "Luchini" might not have belonged to Camp Lo, but another successful associate of Ski's.

"Jay-Z heard 'Luchini,'" remembers the producer. "He wanted it, but I couldn't give it to him. You see, 'Feelin' It' was originally a Camp Lo beat, but I gave it Jay. To make up for 'Feelin' It,' Camp Lo got 'Luchini.' I was going through that, like, every day. Every beat I made, artists were like, 'Yo, I want that! I want that!'"

Although the thought of Jay-Z murdering the orchestra hits and junkyard drums of this fabled beat is somewhat of a rap fantasy, Ski knows he made the right decision. "[Jay] couldn't have did it like Lo. No way. Camp Lo—that's them. They murdered that shit. That shit still sounds crazy."

Ski is always prepared to find the next crazy sample. When the energy wanes, Ski creates a musical diversion by shouting, "Camp Lo! New Camp Lo!"—doing his best hip-hop radio-jock impersonation as he lowers the stylus onto another mysterious LP. If the track is hot, Ski might run a few arpeggios on his trusty air piano. All these studio antics get the group relaxed, yet comfortably focused, eager to see what kind of sonic fate lay in the next hand of cards.

"I'm a Virgo, so I be kind of studying past Virgo movements," claims Cheeba, who favors star charts to the luck of the draw. Cheeba honors Barry White, Michael Jackson, and Roy Ayers as some of his favored astrological brethren. "We was in the studio with Doug E. Fresh—who's also a Virgo—and he was basically telling [Pittsburgh] Slim, who's a Virgo, and Ski, who's a Virgo, certain things. His Virgo advice was like, 'Don't overanalyze shit—sometimes you can hold yourself back from greatness.' He was saying, as a Virgo, he does that, but, for the most part, you just got to let your hands go. I just recently started letting my hands go last year—like not really caring about little stuff. Ten years ago, I *really* didn't care. But then, a lot of times, after being fucking stuck in bullshit paperwork, you start caring about bullshit—and it changes your whole mood. So now I say, 'Fuck it—what's the worst that could happen?'"

So now, two albums and ten years later, Camp Lo, along with producers Ski and Juice, will try to use a potent brew of cosmic energy, raw talent, aged wisdom, and good old-fashioned fate to write the next chapter in the Camp Lo saga. They may very well be on their own planets, but we need them down here on Earth. ○

Guilty Simpson

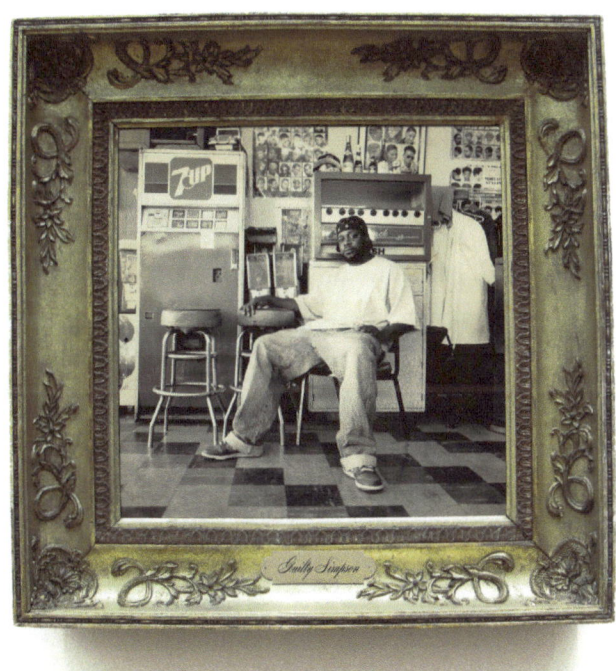

Ode to the Ghetto
Stones Throw Records
www.stonesthrow.com

COLLECTIVE VIBRATIONS

L.A.'s Build an Ark manifests peace through music

text
Andy Thomas

photography
B+

"The idea of Build an Ark was firstly a way of me saying to those creative people around me that they should come together and do it themselves," explains bandleader and lynchpin of this cross-generational L.A. soul-jazz collective, Carlos Niño, from his home in Echo Park. "I was also trying to refer to how Sun Ra and Horace Tapscott had continued the tradition of the big bands of Duke Ellington and Fletcher Henderson, and to show how important that model is for the community today."

When they recorded their debut outing, *Peace with Every Step*, it was as a direct response to the fear and confusion following 9/11. Since then, this amalgam of disparate yet like-minded spirits has continued to grow and to spread its message of peace and love to an ever more troubled world. Build an Ark brings together elders like Derf Reklaw of Chicago jazz-funk ensemble the Pharoahs; Phil Ranelin, cofounder of Detroit's legendary Tribe Records; and spiritual jazz vocalist Dwight Trible, with young heads from L.A.'s various underground scenes, such as Plug Research's Damon Aaron and Niño's partner in Life Force Trio, Dexter Story.

Build an Ark's ethos of communality was inspired both by the Leimert Park arts movement, which burst into life in South Central L.A. during the Rodney King uprisings, and the radical jazz cooperatives of the late '60s and early '70s, from Tribe and Black Jazz through to Strata East and AACM. "The name is all about community and the idea that if we build our own ship, we can collectively transcend into a higher awareness and creativity," states Niño assuredly. "That kind of thinking is what brings about change, and our world is in real need of healing change."

Back in 1956, Afro-futurist Sun Ra proclaimed: "In tomorrow's world, men will not need artificial instruments such as jets and space ships. In the world of tomorrow, the new man will 'think' the place he wants to go, then his mind will take him there." An avid collector of Ra's material, Niño remains a firm believer in his musical mysticism and the power of collective energy. "The whole idea of the Arkestra was for a vessel to awaken spiritual vibrations. Everything is vibrational. The idea of the Ark as I see it is that together we can tune to a higher frequency and connect to the real essence of our potential as creative beings."

Although he is careful to avoid any comparisons with the great astral traveler, Carlos does share the same commitment to his creative ensemble. "I can only say that it's obvious to me that Ra was inspired by a magnificent energy. And that inspiration allowed him to endure. I find myself tested regularly in that sense. So, I look to him to stay connected to that wondrous vibration."

A. ANDRES RENTERIA
B. MIGUEL ATWOOD-FERGUSON
C. RALPH "BUZZY" JONES
D. DERF REKLAW
E. DEXTER STORY
F. DAMON ARRON
G. CARLOS NIÑO
H. GABY HERNANDEZ
I. MARK MAXWELL
J. DWIGHT TRIBLE
K. NICK ROSEN
L. PHIL RANELIN

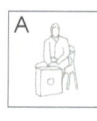
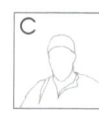
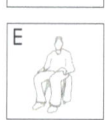

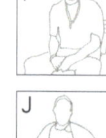
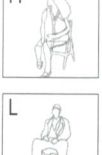
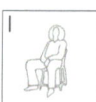
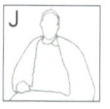

When Niño started uniting the jazz and hip-hop communities through his Spaceways radio show on KPFK in 2001, it was as an eighteen-year-old whose energy and vision inspired all those around him. He takes his role as a connecter and instigator very seriously. "When it's your job to organize lots of people for something great and revolutionary, you face all sorts of trying situations. So you have to be inspired by something beautiful to persevere. It takes focus, diligence, and love."

While *Peace with Every Step* was recorded over a two-day period, its follow-up is a more reflective affair, with the free Build an Ark sound given more depth and texture. "*Dawn* had been brewing in my mind and heart for a long time," states the tireless producer, who still finds time to drop science as one half of Ammoncontact. "I was trying hard to find financing for it so that I could get more players together in a better recording studio. So this record was better planned and focused. Even more so on a conceptual level than with *Peace with Every Step*. The whole recording is meant to sound like the dawn, and I feel that it does."

I put it to Niño that the major development on this second release is the more organic instrumentation, from the piano of Nate Morgan (original member of Horace Tapscott's Pan Afrikan People's Arkestra) to the celestial harp of Rebekah Raff. "These were very important elements," agrees Carlos. "The acoustic energy was essential this time, and the whole approach and follow through were more textural." Central to the coloring is string arranger Miguel Atwood-Ferguson, one of the many rising stars of the collective who Carlos tells me has just been brought in to work with Dr. Dre. "He really stepped up with his incredible creativity and musical direction," Niño enthuses. "The strings were expanded from the first record, and his contribution was stellar. He really brought a lot to the project. Just wait until you hear more of his work!"

Another master musician on the album is Big Black, the unsung hand drummer whose congas and distinctive African percussion were featured on such landmark jazz outings as Freddie Hubbard's *Blue Spirits*, Doug Carn's *Adam's Apple*, and Randy Weston's *African Cookbook*. "He is one of the greatest rhythm players of all time," states Niño, who is again responsible for introducing younger ears to the music of another of jazz music's cult figures. "Everyone should check his records from the '60s and '70s on UNI," he says. (Check the heavy sounds and cover art of *Message to Our Ancestors* and *Elements of Now* from '67 and '68.) "Here is another player who has been hugely influential, though people don't really know him like they should. Adam Rudolph [the multi-percussionist and Don Cherry collaborator who is a key member of the BAA family and Hu Vibrational, another of Niño's projects] and Mtume were his two main disciples. Word up! He's really amazing."

A majestic version of Big Black's "Love, Sweet Like Sugar Cane" is one of the well-chosen covers on an album that sees Carlos developing his songwriting skills, such as on the Black Jazz–style vocal of the title track. "The chant section and meditative part of 'Dawn' were in my head for a long time—since we recorded *Peace with Every Step*. I sat down with Miguel at the piano and sang it to him over and over until we had it fully written out. Then he added some beautiful chords on the second section, and I thought to have it vamp-out in the middle."

The progression of Niño and his musical family as they discover new oceans of creativity is testament both to the bandleader's vision and passion, as well as the mutual belief and trust of the ensemble. Radical and relevant, Build an Ark is beginning to justify its place in the jazz canon alongside those collectives that first inspired the young Carlos.

As he continues to give props to others on this project, such as Avotcja, original singer with Horace Tapscott's vocal troupe U.G.M.A.A., it is clear that his drive remains as strong today as when he programmed live shows by Yusef Lateef and Saul Williams as a young enthusiast back in the day. "We are one, together. It's an illusion to think that we're not connected. So, the importance of the collective is to broaden our channel of love. Just like light particles, we come together to shine even brighter. Musically and spiritually, it's constant. The collective is our life, and all we want to do is make heart music that will inspire others to get together and transform." ●

Build an Ark's *Dawn* is out now on vinyl by Kindred Spirits.

Juan Pablo Torres

FORBIDDEN FRUITS

Castro's Communist Cuba proves fertile ground for experimental music scene

text by & photos courtesy of
Pablo Ellicott Yglesias

The musical environment in Castro's Cuba over the last half century has been a unique bundle of contradictions and circumstances. Cuban musicians have been creating vital and challenging music in a schizophrenic atmosphere of State support and suppression, isolation and international influence, shortages of materials and a surplus of talent; and it is their unique sociopolitical circumstances, coupled with incredible skill, drive, and determination, that has helped create a body of music unlike any other in the world, let alone on the Latino music scene. Through all the changes in economic situations or shifting relations with Russia or the United States, Cubans have never let music become simply a consumer product, even during the heightened times of Buena Vista Social Club activity (the "special period" of Cuban music, as it were). Music has remained a vital collective practice and a form of social identity, closely tied with African practices of communal participation and religious and cultural activity, and serving the dual purposes of social and political expression.

Carlos Alfonso, composer, bassist, and founder and leader of the soul/rock/Afro-Cuban/fusion group Síntesis, and not a fan of the Buena Vista Social Club phenomenon, has said: "The painter and the musician reflects the situation of the country… Music here is not about romance and play and entertainment." Juan de Marcos González, who as a young man played funk and rock guitar and later exchanged his Sly Stone and Beatles licks for a traditional Cuban tres guitar in 1976, went on to cofound the acoustic *son típico* group Sierra Maestra in 1977, which was a radical move at the time for a young Afro-wearing, bell-bottomed soul-rocker. Most recently, de Marcos González founded and became director of the Afro-Cuban All Stars, and, most famously, producer of the Buena Vista Social Club sessions. In an interview, he summed up the Cuban socio-musical situation succinctly:

> Cuba is a poor country. We have nothing, but we have the music. We are proud of the music. We are proud to be Cubans. And this is a very happy country, even if we are completely fucked over. But we are happy. That's the problem of the Cubans. We are Latinos and half African, so we can make a joke about our problems. It's normal to find a lot of jokes in the streets about our own problems.

That said, the Revolution contributed to this de-emphasizing of commercial concerns by making every musician an employee of the state: giving all musicians an opportunity to achieve higher education; providing venues without the dues-paying system prevalent elsewhere; and doing away with practices like payola and exploitative record labels with bogus contracts. Though the opportunity to make supplementary money outside the country is forbidden, and suppression and censorship have always been a part of the government's way of regulating and attempting to control careers and the creative process, many incredible bands and musicians have been able to create fabulous music without competition or commercial concerns. Who can say what kind of music might have been produced had the old systems stayed intact. We all know about the musicians like Paquito d'Rivera who eventually left because their careers were stifled and conditions were unbearable for them, but a lot of great music was made before exile became a solution for them, and many other talented musicians have stayed. Suffice it to say that despite blockades, ostracism, shortages, surveillance, and various arbitrary government controls, Cuban musicians do receive first-rate educations, never go hungry, and continue to be innovative and influential the world over, though politics and history have made it difficult for their music to be known on a larger scale in the States for the most part, until recently.

It is interesting to note that while many post-Revolutionary youth in Cuba were soaking up English-language pop music like the Beatles, Cream, Jimi Hendrix, James Brown, Sly and the Family Stone, and Pink Floyd, as well as more Latin-flavored groups like Santana and War, there was also a counter movement that tried to preserve roots music, but connect it more to the young, which eventually fed into an officially sanctioned genre called *nueva trova* that was akin to international protest folk but also espoused the revolutionary ideals of the Socialist Party line. Though some contend nueva trova formed a musical tyranny of sorts for a decade, and many musicians were threatened or imprisoned for playing "subversive" music like acid rock, the leading lights of the genre were often backed by musicians who loved jazz, rock, and funk. There was definitely a small, experimental electronic and jazz scene, and many pop groups got away with lyrics that sported double meanings that eluded the censors. Interestingly, these groups also incorporated "foreign" sounds like electronics, funk, rock, and R&B in innovative ways that endeared them to some of the public. Most ostensibly, Latin dance records of the '70s in Cuba sported at least one experimental or odd-sounding track; finding the hidden funk cuts can be an entertaining game for the intrepid break-monger. These days, Cuban popular dance music seems not so stunningly innovative in terms of inventing new genres out of whole cloth like the way Los Van Van invented *songo* in the '70s. Now there seems to be a lot of grafting of genres going on; reggae and rap have of course made inroads, and as the recent film *Habana Blues* attests, there are death metal and punk bands operating on the fringes of the current music scene.

Beatdiggers are always looking for the illest breaks you never heard, from yodeling Turkish funkadelia to forgotten Ethio-jazz 45s. Recent discoveries in Colombia, Panama, Barbados, and Belize thicken the Caribbean *criollo* flavoring of global dusty grooves, but Cuba is curiously absent from the limelight, though she's been right there under our noses all along. In the '80s and early '90s, David Byrne and Ned Sublette were the first Anglos to expose average Americans to the funkier side of the Gran Caimán (the island is said to resemble a big crocodile) when they laid on an unsuspecting general public such monstrous jams as "Bacalao con Pan" by Irakere and "Llegué, Llegué/Guararé de Pastorita" by Los Van Van. Though the American public was largely kept from being exposed to post-Revolution music, plenty of salsa musicians, especially in South America and Puerto Rico, were influenced by or covered contemporary Cuban dance tunes.

Funky Cuba

Irakere

Los Van Van

Grupo Monumental

ICAIC

Puerto Rico's premier '80s fusion group, Batacumbele, was completely enmeshed in *songo*; cover versions of tunes from behind the Sugar Cane Curtain ranged from Los Reyes '73's "Baila que Baila" done by Típica '73, to Rubén Blades's smokin' "Muevete," originally by Los Van Van. However, for the most part, the funkiest or most experimental stuff remained buried treasure. That is, until 2006, when an intrepid Canadian DJ by the name of Dan Zachs compiled *Sí, para Usted (The Funky Beats of Revolutionary Cuba, Volume 1)* on his Waxing Deep label.

What is so unique about the music coming out of Cuba in the '70s is that it really had nothing to do with the salsa scenes in New York City, Puerto Rico, or South America. The blockade imposed by the United States effectively cut off all direct contact with El Norte, and travel between the two markets dried up, so New York Latin developed in a vacuum using the old pre-Castro models of mambo, son, and guaracha. Granted, progressive innovators like Willie Colón, Eddie Palmieri, Larry Harlow, Conjunto Libre, Cortijo, and Roberto Roena were not slavishly emulating the great Cuban bands of the '50s completely; they played with a harder, grittier urban sound, and also looked inward to indigenous styles like *jíbaro*, *bomba*, and *plena*, as well as looking outward and taking elements of the soul, funk, jazz, and rock worlds surrounding them. But as far as those New York cats evolving in crazy directions like them Cubans back on their island, no way, José, it wasn't happening; there was commercial pressure in the U.S. to play dance music within certain traditional norms. Some Stateside musicians copped an attitude about the poor quality of Cuban instruments or production values at EGREM, the State recording agency, so the disconnect was profound on some levels. Meantime, Cubans steadfastly followed their own path—censorship or not—equally cut off but more adventurous in their own way, incorporating strange electronics, film soundtracks, cheesy effects, Eastern European jazz, developments in African pop, and bizarre vocalizing. And somehow, especially in the music of Juan Pablo Torres, Irakere, and early Los Van Van, a *lot* of funky beats got laid down.

Some of the members of the best young groups of the '70s got their start by playing in orchestras set up by older jazz musicians or government institutions as part of new nation-building efforts after the Revolution. The most notable of these institutions was the Cuban Institute for Movie-Making, Art, and Industry (ICAIC), which in 1970 founded the Grupo de Experimentación Sonora del ICAIC (the Experimental Sound Group of the ICAIC). The band, deliberately given a noncommercial name, was a collective of musicians led by Leo Brouwer, an accomplished classical guitarist from an illustrious musical family and a professor from the National School of the Arts. Under Brouwer, the Grupo de Experimentación Sonora embodied, perhaps more than any other band or musician, the creativity and artistic license of the period. Officially, they were charged with producing soundtracks for Cuban cinema, but the musicians were free to choose projects as they pleased and often composed tracks for imaginary films. They had tremendous independence and the members took full advantage of it to expand Cuban music, often backing singer/songwriters like Pablo Milanés or Silvio Rodriguez. Rooting their compositions in traditional Cuban forms, the Grupo de Experimentación Sonora explored what they felt were the best elements from international music. Their influences were eclectic, spanning Brazilian tropicália, electronic music, jazz, funk, folk, and psychedelic rock. The other important early group that served as a training ground and crucible of modern approaches to Cuban popular music was Orquesta Cubana de Música Moderna, founded by jazz trap drummer Guillermo Barreto, Carlos Emilio, and Irakere's pianist Jesus "Chucho" Valdés. Valdés stated the open-minded philosophy of the times best: "Fusion is universalization. Historically, all music was formed this way, by enriching itself through outside influences. You must listen to everything, so you can define yourself as a composer, and that's the most difficult thing."

One important thing to remember when studying the freaky '70s in Cuba is the indisputable fact that Cuban music has *always* had the funk, long before Juan Formell first plucked his electric bass or Changuito mashed together a timbale set and traps, because it's always had that *African* heritage. Street rumba and Santería drumming have some of the most incredibly complex and nasty rhythms in the world, and you might say the original break-dancers were the *rumberos* (rumba dancers) in the Black communities of Havana and Matanzas. Many a Habanero has said: "*Coño, compadre,* if James Brown were Cuban, he would be like Arsenio Rodríguez and Beny Moré rolled into one!" That is to say, long before Los Van Van's incredibly funky drummer José Luis "Changuito" Quintana was doing mad Tony Allen and Clyde Stubblefield beats in the '70s, the son montunos and mambos of Arsenio, Beny, and Cachao were some of the stickiest gutbucket get-down dance forms around.

The following are some brief bios of the players on the funky side of thangs in Cuba, from the '60s to the '80s. On a visual tip, the album cover art was pretty different too, coming across like a mix of backwater tropical pulp fiction paperback art and Eastern European Communist–era movie posters high on rum and cigar smoke.

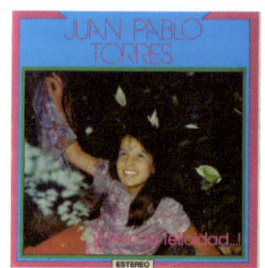

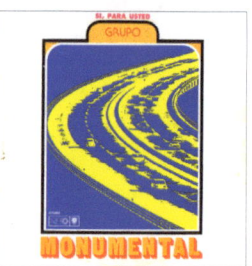
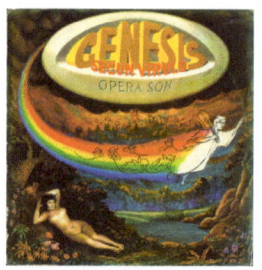

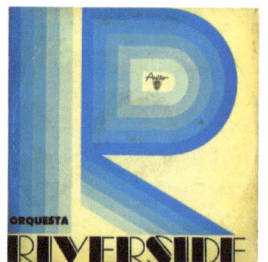

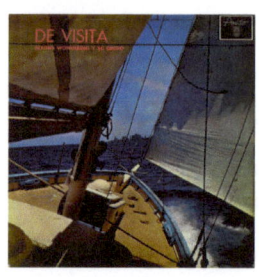

Funky Cuba

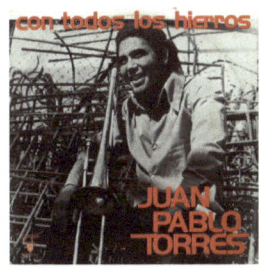  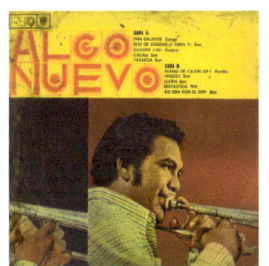 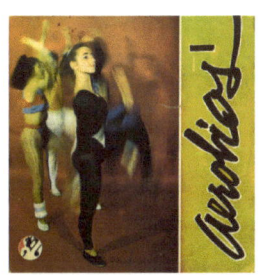

 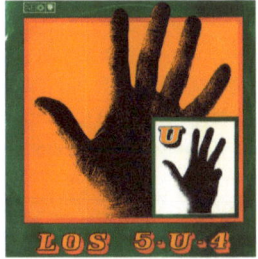  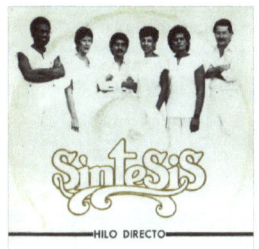
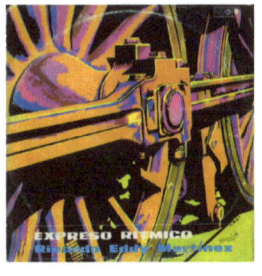   

 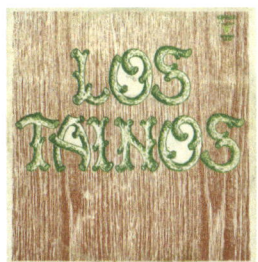  

Grupo Irakere Formed in Havana in 1973, the band has recorded some of the most innovative, rocking Afrocentric jazz and dance music ever. "Irakere," in the Lucumí religion and Yoruba language, means "forest," and this band comes across like the jungle groove for the electronic age. Members have included Jesús "Chucho" Valdés, Paquito d'Rivera, Arturo Sandoval, and Carlos Averoff, among others. As Chucho always says, "Irakere is a style." Best albums: their 1974 debut, *Irakere* (blue cover, Areito 3420), and 1978's *Irakere* (red cover, Areito 3926).

Los Van Van Though they share a name with the new-wave group the Go-Go's, these are the cats who really have the beat. When bassist Juan Formell left the orchestra of Elio Revé to form Van Van in 1969, he took most of the band with him. From the get-go, he started messing with the old charanga flute/violin format, making some pretty out-there bubble gum at first. By the time "Changuito" was transforming the beats into funk, the group sported a low-down sound of electric organ and flute that really got nasty in the mid-'70s. You want the LP where the band is all in striped suits (Areito 3471, 1975). In F or VG condition, that baby could cost you a few pints of blood!

Ricardo Edy Martínez The track "Adeoey" from the LP Los Reyes '73 has received far more acclaim from contemporary funk collectors than it ever did in Cuba, where this relatively obscure track never garnered much attention. This is not surprising; guitarist and arranger Ricardo Eddy Martínez points the uncredited musicians well into the left-field of electronics and psychedelia, so much so that this track sounds nothing like the rest of their album. Other tunes off the album like "Baila que Baila" were highly influential among salsa musicians in the United States and Puerto Rico. EGREM, Cuba's one and only record label since the Revolution, would occasionally commission an album in order to diversify and improve the catalog of Cuban music. Expresso Rítmico from producer Martínez was such an album. We don't know whether EGREM was pleased with the whole LP, some of it being derivative disco, but they were surely impressed by "Tambó Iya," with its throaty yells for "más batá," the sacred drums used in Santería rituals. This is another track far better known amongst the DJs of North America, Europe, and Japan than in Cuba.

Síntesis This long-lived (since 1975) and eclectic conglomeration started out as Cuba's first prog-rock band, influenced by Pink Floyd, Yes, and ELP, but they soon mutated into a fusion of rock, jazz, disco-funk, and traditional Cuban music. The vocals often remind one of Sergio Mendes or Flora and Airto records. They are now best known for their *Ancestros* albums, which blend the traditional chants and beats of Santería with synthesizers and guitars. Síntesis is highly regarded in Cuba, but the funky track "Con la Luz de la Mañana" (from their 1984 LP *Hilo Directo*) in particular has become something of a hit in European modern-soul sets.

Juan Pablo Torres Trombonist, composer, and all-around genius J. P. Torres, whose death at fifty-nine in 2005 was a tremendous blow to lovers of great music the world over, was one of the most prolific and experimental Cuban artists of the '70s and '80s. J.P. worked as a producer for EGREM, his crowning achievement there being the five *Estrellas de Areíto* albums. He later moved to the United States, where he cut many tasty jazz sides in New York and Florida. Torres began his adult career with the Orquesta Cubana de Música Moderna, a group whose influence was similar to the Grupo de Experimentación Sonora because of its innovative material and role as a training ground for luminaries like d'Rivera, Chucho Valdés, Gonzalo Rubalcaba, and Arturo Sandoval. Later, Torres formed the de facto studio band Algo Nuevo to explore and develop Cuban music (public venues and television at the time were not equipped with the appropriate technical resources to allow the band to play live with all their electronics). "I have always known what I wanted to do," he told interviewer Linda Lovit. "Even though I listen to and perform jazz, my identity is Creole—the music I was born with. I became aware of the incredible strength of Cuban music at a very young age. Using it as a base, I'm able to branch out in any direction." His best tracks deploy an astoundingly innovative fusion of electronics, funk, fuzz, and son (check out Algo Nuevo's crisp drummers, Amadito Valdés and Filiberto Sánchez). Must-have albums are a pair of funky gems from 1977: *Con Todo los Hierros* and *Súper-son*. Both are now available on a single CD from Malanga Music. ⬤

Resources
Liner notes for *Sí, para Usted (The Funky Beats of Revolutionary Cuba, Volume 1)*, compiled by Dan Zachs (Waxing Deep Records, 2006, www.waxingdeep.org).
Liner notes for Algo Nuevo by J. P. Torres
(new CD reissue on Malanga Music, Andorra, 2007).
Cuban Music from A to Z by Helio Orovio (Duke University Press, 2004).
Dancing With Fidel by Stephen Foehr (Sanctuary Publishing, 2001).
The Rough Guide to Cuban Music by Phillip Sweeney (Rough Guides Ltd., 2001).
Cuban Fire: The Story of Salsa and Latin Jazz by Isabelle Leymarie (Continuum, 2002).
Cuban Music by Maya Roy (Markus Wiener, 2002).

HOMENAJE
BROWNOUT
CD/LP

Debut album from Austin's filthiest purveyors of deep fried dirty Texas funk. Consisting of members of Grupo Fantasma and Ocote Soul Sounds, this stunning album features the huge selling singles "Homenaje" and "African Battle" alongside 11 more Latin infused gems.

"Restores my faith that all may not be lost. Technically on-point yet fun and groovy as hell, if this doesn't get the party started y'all must be DOA!"
Toph One, XLR8R magazine

"Santeros Funk, I am converted!"
Will Holland, Quantic Soul Orchestra

OUT NOW!

FREESTYLE

IT REMAINS TO BE SEEN
AFRO ELEMENTS
CD

The debut album from the musical force behind Mr Gone's live set up and a studio tour-de-force. Deep jazz, funk and soul flavours all rolled into one smooth ride. Features the singles 'It Remains To Be Seen' and 'Think'.

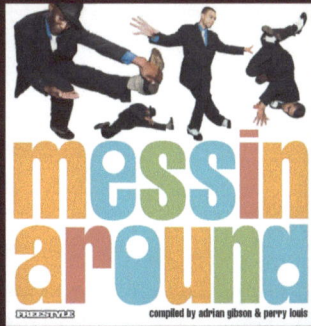

MESSIN AROUND
VARIOUS ARTISTS
CD/12" SAMPLER

Volume 5 of the popular jazz-dance compilation, celebrating eleven exhilarating years at the Jazz Café. With exclusive tracks by Grupo X, Sheila Landis, Art Ensemble of Camden and Jazz Juice.

MODERN FUNK
VARIOUS ARTISTS
CD/2 x 7" SAMPLERS

Volume 3 of the hugely successful 'Stay On The Groove' compilation series, featuring tracks from Mark Ronson, Sharon Jones & The Dap Kings, Quantic and Speedometer.

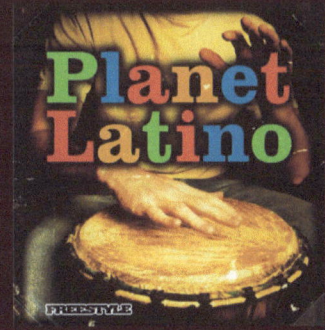

PLANET LATINO
VARIOUS ARTISTS
CD/12" SAMPLER

15 tracks of Latin dancefloor heat, hispanic hip-shakers and heavy hitting salsa dura, descarga and mambo. Featuring tracks from Aloe Blacc, Luisito Quintero, Sirius B and Bobby Matos.

FREESTYLE

WWW.FREESTYLERECORDS.CO.UK

THE STRATEGIST

text Matt Rogers

Fabled soul commander Mighty Hannibal plays both ends against the middle

"I learned how to do what this society taught me, and that's play both ends against the middle," states the one and only James T. Shaw, better known in musical circles as Hannibal, both Mighty and King. When he's holding court, best advised to fasten your seat belt.

"See, back in them days, if you're Black, they'd give you two suits, a Cadillac, and a White woman. I didn't want none of that; I just wanted my money. Then I could buy my own car and have *two* White ladies!"

And keep it fastened.

"Record labels are full of shit. They call it R&B. Rhythm is one music, blues is another music. Like when I was first coming up as a kid, I was 'colored.' Well, I can't speak 'colored'! Then I was 'negro'; I can't speak 'negro'! What's that mean? It means 'black' in Spanish! Well, hell, I ain't Spanish! That's the same with the music biz. They talk about blues and jazz; jazz ain't nothing but the blues that you *jazzed* up. Ain't no such thing as rhythm and blues—it's the *blues!*"

Hannibal is nothing if not outspoken, his crackly Southern drawl cartoonish in its gruffness, his propensity for detail frightening, blunt, poetic. Maybe you've never heard of him, but he'll tell you—from Hotlanta to the City of Angels to the Big Apple and back—he was there.

As we sit in his austere South Bronx apartment, the sixty-eight-year-old singer and self-proclaimed father of "message music" makes no apologies for who he is or for who he's been, the latter a list that could make your momma cry. His stories certainly will. Ask him about being driven around L.A., Ray Charles behind the wheel, looking to score dope; about Sam Cooke beating his ass, then taking him to BMI in his Jaguar to set up his Captain Music publishing company; taking karate lessons from organist Jimmy Smith *and* Chuck Norris; or renting and riding a Ringling Bros. elephant down Broadway in a green turban and suit (the $200 fine for not having the proper "pooper scooper" well worth the free publicity garnered later that night via Cronkite and Brinkley). He's happy to share.

"Black people abandoned their music, so young White people took it up. The reason I'm working today is not because of Black people—and I *love* my people—but because White people remember your history. Black people remember the last three minutes you was on the radio. My audience now, their grandmas bought my music. I'm packing my house with nothing but young White kids, and it's nothing but the blues, man." True enough, despite the glaucoma that blinded him several years ago, the White kids keep this Atlanta-born ex-pimp workin' the stage he loves, though when the showbiz bug bit him as a teenager, it was the Black kids who gave him that first push.

These days, gathering Hannibal on original vinyl requires a few bills, but, thankfully, an excellent anthology, *Hannibalism!*, from Norton Records, showcases the buttery-voiced singer/composer/producer's multi-genre, multi-label run through the music game from '58 to '73, including his prescient hit, "Hymn No. 5," a song still resonant today. And then there's his only long player, *Truth*, a hellafied funk bomb from '72 featuring Atlanta mates Hermon Hitson, Lee Moses, Freddie Terrell, and his wife, singer Delia Gartrell.

All the above are just a few of the folks Hannibal can yarn on about if you let him, down to the color of their wardrobe and refreshment of choice on a given day. If you listen long enough, you'll sputter away, convinced the man's never met a dull moment he couldn't whup.

Hannibal: Let me say that anybody in the state of Georgia named Collins, Shaw, Roberts, Ferrell, Jordan is akin to me. When I was four, I started singing in church. My father was a piano player, and, in those days, whoever had the piano had a house party on Saturday night. So that was my first taste. And then I was listening to folks like Hank Ballard, the "5" Royales, Marie Adams, Junior Parker, and country music on the radio. Sometimes, I'd slip into the shows.

In high school, I had a doo-wop group called the Overalls, which included Ed Patten and Merald Knight, Gladys's brother. We'd sing, dance, and wear overalls. Well, on Stunt Night at Washington High School, we won first prize; I did a dance called the Itch and turned it out! So I told my daddy, "I wanna go into show biz." The next day, [he] got me outta bed and said, "Okay, we're gonna go to your job." He took me to where he worked, gave me a pitchfork, a shovel, and I had to dig dirt. Man, by 12:00 P.M., I was so tired I went back to school. [*laughs*] But then, Jack "the Rapper" Gibson, a DJ at WERD in Atlanta, allowed us to come sing at the station, [and] I got bit by the bug real good. So I put my age up to join the Army to get out of Georgia. Ed and Merald became the Pips.

What year?

Fifty-six. [But] I couldn't escape Georgia for shit. I went to jump school—jumped out of airplanes. It was during integration, but it was bullshit. All them cats in the National Guard was getting promoted—the weekend soldiers I called them. I'd been there every day for nine months, so I went AWOL.

My daddy convinced me to turn myself in, so when I got back, I got extra duty, cutting grass with scissors, so I left. [Finally] they gave me an honorable discharge: "Inadaptable for military life," so I get my benefits today! Even bought a house in Compton on my GI Bill.

Damn, you were a player!
To the bone! When I got back from the Army, I decided I'd sing by myself. Got to California around '57, '8, met Sam Cooke, Lou Rawls, Ed Townsend—

Hold on, why California?
Go West, young man! Stuck it out in a car for six weeks before finding a job and apartment right across from the L.A. Coliseum and the Stadium Club, where all entertainers used to try and get gigs. So when I met Johnny Otis and told him I was lookin', he says, "Can you sing?" Arrogant, [I] says, "I ain't no amateur!" [He says,] "Prove it! I'm having a talent show, twenty-five-dollar prize; you win, you've got a job." So I proceeded to knock fire, sang "Please, Please, Please," and got the job. Stayed with Johnny about seven months. Jimmy Nolen played guitar. Was on Shindig; Bob Eubanks was the host. See, back in those days, this business was controlled by a clique—five Jewish families in New York City.

Who didn't get you your first record deal.
No. First was "Big Chief Hug-um an' Kiss-um" under Jimmy Shaw. I hates to hear it. I couldn't sing, couldn't even talk! That was Kent Harris, Concept Records. He was the first person who taught me how to write. His sister, Betty Harris, was married to Redd Foxx. I was sleeping in their broom closet.

How'd you come up with the name Hannibal?
Aki Aleong, from All My Children, gave me the name in '59. He also had Pan World Records. At that time, there were too many Jimmys: Jimmy Reed, McCracklin, Clanton…so I had one name, like Fabian and Dion. Hannibal stuck.

[We listen to some of Hannibal's earlier singles, for example, "Motha Goose Breaks Loose," "My Name Is Hannibal"]

Silliest shit in the world! Hurts my ears. [*laughs*] Man, some of them songs, if you didn't have a copy, you'd never hear it. I didn't copyright it; I hoped they'd steal it, so I could say, "I know nothing about it!" I was just doing what everyone else was doing, trying to keep my record out. Like throwin' shit on the wall, some of it gonna stick.

See, Little Richard was hot. Everyone was trying to sound like him, including me. Met him in '58. Richard is a very unique, most misunderstood individual. Dogged real bad. Took all the bullshit from all who followed. It was race music. Every time Richard cut a hit, Pat Boone had to cut it, 'cause they didn't want White people listening to Black music. Elvis killed all that shit, hung around Blacks, so they finally let Blacks through. But rock and roll was created by Little Richard Penniman. Chuck Berry, Fats Domino—they came after.

Then there was Ike and Tina. I was on tour with them. Tina was a trooper. We'd [be] strugglin', eatin' baloney sandwiches, but Tina was tough. They and the Ikettes was the baddest. And then the hippies like Salvatore Bono and Cher walking around with bearskin rugs on in the summertime. Glen Campbell had a guitar with four strings on it. And Herb Albert had that coronet in a brown paper sack. [*laughs*] Everybody was scramblin'.

How long did it take you to make money from your music?
Back in them days, I didn't have my music-business head on. Brother, I was just trying to stay in the limelight. Me, Little Johnny Taylor, and Lowell Fulsom were playing [places like] Moe's Swing Club, making fifteen dollars a night and had to divide it. Same with H. B. Barnum, Jimmy Norman, Charles Wright. [laughs] All I was interested in doing was pimpin' hoes and singing on the weekend. At one time, I had ten: I was serious busy. And each one had a quota of one hundred dollars a day. See, me, Johnny "Guitar" Watson—piano was his instrument; the man's hands were as fast as Oscar Peterson's—and Larry Williams worked together pimpin' and had too many of them young girls up in Hollywood, so they decided they'd blackball us out of the [music] business if we didn't quit.

How did you get into that business?
It's gotta be in ya. To me, a so-called pimp—a *player*—you can't just wake up and do that. See, my granddaddy was a player. It was just in me. And that is one part of my life I regret, especially when I started having daughters—I had to stop!

So you left L.A., went to Atlanta, then New York City, and, by 1966, you were wearing a turban.
I started wearing a turban 'cause everybody was wearin' Afros, and it went with my name. When I first went back to Atlanta around '65, I had a turban and a harem girl with [a] veil. Little Richard came to my show and sat in, said, "Hannibal, go get you a limou*sine*! So he calls a funeral home, asks

me, "Can you afford fourteen dollars a night?" I says, "Send it on!" When I got a limo, my crowd picked up six hundred percent. Richard was at the Domino Lounge, and I was at the Kitten's Corner, and we were among the first Black people to integrate clubs in Atlanta. I had my drummer Dennis St. John's band [of Neil Diamond fame], a totally White band.

I became the most feared entertainer. I played a gig with James Brown for ten days, kicked his ass like it was a cheese sandwich. Him, Otis [Redding], they did not want to appear with me, 'cause I would tear them a new asshole. They were friends of mine, but business is business. Joe Tex was the only person that didn't fear me. After I had "Hymn No. 5," we played the Apollo, toured together—hell of a dude.

"Hymn No. 5" was your first true hit. Did you call it "message music" then?
Yes. Nina Simone taught me about "message music" more than anyone else. Mama Peaches, I called her. After she wrote "Mississippi Goddamn," I [thought] if a woman could talk like that, then I knew I'm fit to say something. I wrote "Hymn" 'cause I thought [Vietnam] was an unjust war. I wasn't afraid to say shit. Bobby Robinson told me to take out the blood; I said, "Go to hell." Man, everyone was trying to block that record, and it said, "Zoom!" Sold so fast. Then a cat came back from Vietnam with a 45 bootleg on a Saigon label: they were playing it as propaganda over there! [*laughs*] We cut that song in one take, no rehearsal. I was helping produce a Grover Mitchell session, and he had a half hour left in the studio, so I used it.

Then you had the monstrous "Get In the Groove"—
"Get in the Groove," now that was the truth! That sucka was flyin', man!

But then you ditched the turban, changed "Mighty" to "King," and finally put out your first album, *Truth*, which showcased your Atlanta crew: Hitson, Terrell, Moses, your wife, Delia...
Delia was a jazz singer at a place called the Birdcage. Sang so good, I'd get torn up, mesmerized. See, we all went through hard knocks together. I remember when Freddie couldn't carry a tune in a bucket, and Hermon—"I Got That Will," that's a good song. I did records on all these guys. Lee Moses used to live across the street, had a green Kay guitar, a little amp, was bad, funky. "Truth Shall Make You Free"—that's Lee soloing there. Biggest hit since "Hymn No. 5." Japanese bootleg the hell out of it.

Why'd it take so long to get an album deal?
I wanted to get *paid*. Mike Thevis—a Greek fella, the king of pornography in the South, gangster; everyone was scared of him—says to me, "I understand you want $20,000 for this record. It's a good record, but I ain't never give a nigger $20,000." So I say, "You greasy-ass Greek, who the fuck you think you talking to?!" You know what he did? He said, "I like you," and counted out $20,000 just like that. I don't think you should fear death; you gonna die anyway.

Drugs slowed your career. How'd you get hooked?
Listen, they used to put the drug dealer *on* the bus! When I was nineteen, me, Johnny Watson, Larry Williams, we bought our first twenty-five-dollar cap of cocaine and split it. I was never hooked on nothing until 1969 when I got my heroin habit. Got hooked by accident. Mixed some cocaine and some heroin—they called them speedballs—next thing I know… See, I thought my feet was made for runnin' and my nose for smellin', but during that time, my nose started runnin' and my feet started smellin'. Now something is *wrong* with that! I got in a methadone program, but that was just trading the devil for the witch. So I told my wife, "You better stay with your mama for a while," and I went cold turkey. Pukin' up air, man; nose runnin' like a bucket.

I was clean but then started hanging with the wrong crowd during some down years. Started smoking crack in a cigarette, then found out you could put it in a pipe. Hooked fifteen years, only been off it four, but God gave me the strength to step away. So I've been through it, man. I'm blessed I'm still here.

And I wanna start the Mighty Hannibal Show Business Academy. Teach kids to play instruments, learn the business, how to read contracts, talk to the press, respect themselves. Teach these hip-hoppers how to take their pants up outta their ass with the drawers showin', 'cause this is a serious craft, and I'm not gonna let them disrespect it. ○

For more info on the Mighty Hannibal, visit themightyhannibal.com.

JOSÉ JAMES
The Dreamer

Out Now
CD & Ltd edition 180 gsm Vinyl

"José is here to remind us why we love music so much"
— Gilles Peterson

www.brownswoodrecordings.com
www.myspace.com/josejamesquartet

KISSEY ASPLUND
PLETHORA

FEATURING THE DOPE SINGLES:
"WITH YOU"
"CAOS" & "FUSS'N'FIGHT"

RELEASE DATE:
24TH MARCH 08
EXTENDED PLAY VINYL OUT NOW
PRODUCED BY PAPAJAZZ

WWW.R2RECORDS.COM
WWW.MYSPACE.COM/KISSEYASPLUND
INFO@R2RECORDS.COM

KUTIMAN

"PSYCHEDELIC SPACE FUNK ARCHITECT FROM TEL AVIV" (Straight No Chaser)

"BEAUTIFULLY HEAVY" (Turntable Lab)

"MOSTLY PERFECT FOR SUMMER JAMMING PURPOSES" (The Fader)

OUT NOW ON CD / 2LP / DIGITAL
DISTRIBUTED BY RYKO & GROOVE ATTACK
MELTING POT MUSIC

www.mpmsite.com myspace.com/kutiman

THE OUTSIDER

Varitone visionary Eddie Harris's perpetual search for the edges

text
John Kruth

photography
Tom Copi/Michael Ochs Archives/Getty Images

"I had an interesting experience when I was a kid," saxophonist Lenny Pickett of Tower of Power and the Borneo Horns fame recalled. "I was, like, fourteen and used to practice at Bushrod Park in Oakland, over by where the Black Panther headquarters used to be. And, one day, these hoodlums came over and were trying to hold me up and take my horn. One of them had a gun in his belt and showed it to me. But they wanted me to play something for them first, before they took my instrument. I had been sitting in with this high school stage band at the time, and we'd been playing Lee Morgan's 'Sidewinder.' But I only knew the harmony part, so it didn't sound like anything. They said they knew 'Sidewinder,' and that's not 'Sidewinder.' Then I started to play 'Listen Here.' Usually, I only played scales and long tones when I practiced in the park. So these kids came over to listen, because I never played anything that was on the radio before. The hoodlums began to back off a few yards, and I told the kids, 'Look, I gotta get outta here. These guys got a gun; they want to take my horn. Would you help me? I'll grab my horn. You take my case and run to the fence and pass it over to me, and I'll get out of here.' And they did, and I got away. The hoodlums were too cool to run after me. They were gonna walk. So, in a sense, Eddie Harris's 'Listen Here' saved my life, or at least my horn, that afternoon."

It was hard for most folks to peg Eddie Harris, and it seemed like he liked it that way. Some complained his music was too outside, that it wasn't even "jazz." But Harris was hardly a typical jazz musician, although he could blow through the changes on his tenor like Hurricane Ernesto whenever the mood struck.

Born October 20, 1934, to a Cuban father and a mother from New Orleans, Eddie Harris came up singing in the Baptist Church in his hometown of Chicago. When Harris was three, his cousin, Bernice, began teaching him the piano by ear. At DuSable High School, under the tutelage of Captain Walter Dyett (an important educator to the Windy City's aspiring jazz musicians for over twenty-five years), Harris stud-

> "I'VE NEVER BEEN ONE TO LET MY MIND STAGNATE. IF I DIDN'T EXPERIMENT WITH MUSIC, IT WOULD MEAN NOTHING TO ME."

ied vibraphone but soon switched to clarinet and the tenor sax.

By the late '50s, Eddie was drafted into the Army and would tour Germany and France with the Seventh Army Symphony Band (which also featured the talents of Leo Wright, Don Ellis, and his future bandmate Cedar Walton) and took classical saxophone lessons at the Paris Conservatory of Music before returning once more to the States.

Years later, Harris, in an interview with *Down Beat*, explained that playing music was of equal importance to him as breaking new ground. "My mind is always probing for different things and different sounds," he said. "I've never been one to let my mind stagnate. If I didn't experiment with music, it would mean nothing to me."

In his search for new sounds, Harris played saxophone with a bassoon reed and trumpet with a soprano sax mouthpiece. Although he wasn't the first to employ the Selmer Varitone (electric saxophone), Eddie would master the instrument and ultimately produce his own brand of trippy electronica that rivaled masters of the medium, like Morton Subotnik and Wendy Carlos. Then he'd cut some funk numbers with an irresistible groove. The critics, particularly those lacking ears or imagination, didn't get it. They branded him as a "weirdo" or a "sellout." After all, what other jazzman had three million-selling singles to his name? They included "Exodus" (the first jazz single to go gold), "Listen Here," and "Compared to What" with Les McCann. Some of their criticism held water. With over seventy-five records to his name throughout his career, not all of them were great.

"A lot of people thought Eddie's music was weird," his onetime partner, the soul-jazz pianist/singer Les McCann explained. "And it was because he was tryin' everything. But he knew what he was doin' when he was on a stage. He always hired the proper band to back up whatever mood he was in at that time. Eddie simply was a genius. He played everything. He was crazy, you know. Mentally ill! [*laughs*] He was completely the only one like him. The source of where his music came from was one that nobody had ever heard of before. Whatever is out there, musicians will use. They don't necessarily think about electronics. They think in terms of music," Les said, referring to Harris's electric sax. McCann himself delved into the seductive tonal pallet of ARP synthesizers on his album *Layers* back in 1974, creating the auditory equivalent of a lava lamp. "Certain guys will take electron-

ics and play it and make it come out sounding like music."

"You can't explain Eddie Harris," Joel Dorn said, knocking his fist on a desk with each word to emphasize his point. "I met him back in 1961 when I was a disc jockey in Philly. Eddie had his own feel. Like Bo Diddley, he had his own rhythm thing. He wasn't a good musician; he was brilliant. He'd had a hit with 'Exodus,' which crossed over from jazz to R&B to the pop charts. It came outta nowhere. He'd made a couple albums for Vee-Jay, like *Jazz for Breakfast at Tiffany's* [1961] and *Eddie Harris Goes to the Movies* [1962], and then went to Columbia [in 1964], where he cut some really ghastly albums [like *Cool Sax from Hollywood to Broadway*]. Then he came to Atlantic, and that's where he did his great work, like *The In Sound* [1965], which had 'Freedom Jazz Dance' on it." Harris's classic "Freedom Jazz Dance" became an instant jazz standard, covered by over fifty artists, including Miles Davis.

" 'Freedom Jazz Dance' was such a different take on things," Lenny Pickett said. "It was inventive without being unapproachable. He was unafraid of playing simple modal things that had the funk, and he made it work. It wasn't for commercial reasons. That's what he liked doing. It's not a put-on. It's got an incredible sincerity to it. Eddie really had soul."

"[In 1966] he cut a version of 'Listen Here' [which first appeared on *Mean Greens*], but he played electric piano," Joel continued. "It was a cute little commercial jazz thing, but it didn't go. The first week I had come to Atlantic in June of '67, Arif [Mardin] had cut about three days' worth of material with him before he went into the hospital to have dental surgery. He was afraid his embouchure might not be the same, so [he] wanted to put together a stash of music. He didn't know if he'd be able to record again until after he got used to his new teeth. There was a lot of stuff, and I got the impression from Arif that there wasn't anything that really struck him. There was a new engineer, Bruce Tergesen, and our job was to go through piles and piles of sixteen-track tapes and listen to everything and make an album out of it. That was my first assignment during my first week or ten days at Atlantic. There was one piece I liked, a nice little commercial thing called 'Theme in Search of a Movie' that I had Arif add some strings to. Eddie had cut another take of 'Listen Here' on sax, which was twenty-eight minutes long. We listened to it, and it was nice, but Bruce said there's something in here that's really good. He said if we chop this up right, it could be a

real record. So we started working on it. It went from twenty-eight minutes to twenty minutes, to sixteen, to eleven. And we finally got it down to seven minutes and listened back to it, and it was spectacular. I was inexperienced at that time. I wasn't a great mixer or editor. But Bruce got a bead on it and really turned it into something. So we chopped it up and put it together, and I took it to Nesuhi [Ertegun].

"Eddie was playing the electric saxophone," Dorn continued, "but he wasn't the first. Sonny Stitt was. Stitt made an album for Roulette where he played the Varitone sax, but he essentially played a sax that was plugged in. He never did the really creative things with it that Eddie did. Eddie was always comin' up with something new. The beauty of Eddie Harris was that he tried a lot of stuff. Not everything he did worked. But that never stopped him from trying."

"It's a pretty simple gizmo," Lenny Pickett said, describing the inner workings of the electric saxophone. "It's got a circuit in it called a flip-flop that creates an octave. It's a step-down generator that converts the signal into a square wave, and then cuts it in half, and then possibly in half again. It's got some very simple filters on it that allow you to change the timbre of the sound as well, because the result of the square wave coming through after the flip-flop can have a very harsh sound. So the filter takes some of the high frequencies off and makes it a little mellower. He first used a Maestro [electric sax] for a while and then the Selmer. At Montreux, I think he was using the Maestro, because if you watch the video of the performance, he keeps going over to this box to change the sound. With the Selmer, everything was built on the horn, and you could flip the switch with your right hand while you were playing and change the tone. On the original Varitones, all the wires were encased in a brass tube that wound its way around the saxophone. But it was kind of heavy. They didn't make very many of them, but they worked really well. It was a good gizmo, very effective, and he was really creative with it. It allowed him to have a bass accompaniment to what he was playing on his horn at the same time. On "Listen Here," most people think that's a baritone sax, but that's him playing the low notes on the Varitone. It's similar to what conga players do, when they keep the *tumbao* part going underneath while they solo at the same time. He was playing an octave higher than what was usually written for the horn, but you don't even notice it. He just popped the notes out like they're nothing."

"After we put 'Listen Here' together, the album [1967's *The Electrifying Eddie Harris*] came out, and it took off, just like that!" Dorn recalled. "Around that time, I took my first promotional road trip for Atlantic. My first stop was San Francisco, where I talked with disc jockeys and hung out. I had taken an acetate of Aretha's 'Natural Woman' with me and dropped it off with John Hardy, the top R&B jock in the Bay Area at KDIA. I had a couple other acetates with me by David 'Fathead' Newman and Eddie. I went to the distributorship, and there was this guy that ran the warehouse who had some ears. You'd play stuff for him, and he could tell you what was gonna go, and what wasn't. I put on 'Listen Here,' and the guy went [*whistles*]. 'This is a smash,' he said. I called Nesuhi and told him, 'They're goin' nuts over the Eddie Harris cut.' So they made a single out of it. It was a big record. The song charted at about number thirty on the pop charts. There must have been a hundred thousand copies of it playin' on jukeboxes across the country.

"Then I made a good record with Eddie called *Plug Me In* [1967] with Charles Stepney, a legendary arranger from Chicago who did a lot of great jazz and R&B records," Dorn continued. "He was the guy behind Minnie Riperton and Rotary Connection. Then I recorded him live at the Village Gate, which was just so-so. By the time we made the *Silver Cycles* record [1968], I was already getting on his nerves. He was not an easy guy to get along with, and he had a manager who was…quite something. I got halfway through *Silver Cycles* and was thrown off the project, because he said I overdubbed some bongo drums behind his back. There wasn't a bongo drum within a thousand yards of that record! The next thing I knew, Nesuhi called me in [Dorn admittedly was the Bart Simpson of Atlantic Records]. So Arif finished the album. *Silver Cycles* was brilliant. I've used it on a number of compilations over the years.

"At the time, Nesuhi had just met Claude Nobs, who was working for the Swiss tourist board, and decided to put on a small jazz festival. The idea was to get people to come to Montreux and fly Swiss Air. Nesuhi agreed to pay for some of Atlantic's artists to play the festival if, in return, Claude would supply the label with a recording and film of their performances. I asked him who he had in mind, and he said, 'Les McCann,' who had a minor hit at the time called 'With These Hands.' Then he said, 'Let's send Eddie Harris.'

> "HE WOULD GET A HIT, AND THEN HE WOULD DO EVERYTHING IN THE WORLD TO SHOW EVERYBODY WHAT HE WAS ABOUT OTHER THAN THE HIT."

"I was walking from the studio to the office when Eddie was coming from the office to the studio, and we bumped into each other in the hall," continued Dorn. "He had a trumpet with him that had a saxophone mouthpiece. I said, 'What's that?' He said, 'It's my new invention.' Eddie said, 'Listen to this,' and he started to play. It had an interesting sound." Rahsaan Roland Kirk would later borrow the instrument from him, dubbing it the "trumpophone" to record a stellar version of Miles Davis's "Bye, Bye Blackbird" on his 1975 release *The Case of the 3 Sided Dream in Audio Color*. Dorn continued, "I said, 'You're goin' to Montreux, and Les is goin' to Montreux, so why don't you just walk onstage during Les's set. Don't tell him. Just walk onstage and bust into Les's set playin' the blues on your trumpet.' I thought it would be wild, and when people saw him playin' the trumpet with a saxophone mouthpiece, I thought it would be a great little piece of stage business. He said, 'Cool.'

"So everybody went to Montreux, and Eddie went to Les and told him what I had in mind. Eddie said, 'Why don't we just do a set together?' Les said, 'Fine. What d'ya got?' They didn't really rehearse. Clark Terry was also there, and they asked him to come up and play trumpet and do that mumbles thing of his. [*scats*] A few hours before they were set to go on, Clark asked about the bread. There really wasn't any, so he told them, 'If I'm not gettin' paid, I'm not playin'.' Benny Bailey, an expatriate trumpet player from Cleveland who had been gigging around Europe, was there, and they asked him to join them. His thing was high notes, like Maynard Ferguson. So they did the set with Les's band with Eddie and this trumpet player. There was no rehearsal."

"I had met Eddie before [our historic performance at Montreux on June 21, 1969] and heard about him for years," Les recollected. "One night, we were both in Cleveland, so I stopped in and heard him in person. A few years later, we happened to be on the same label, and Joel made the suggestion that we play together as we were going to be in Switzerland together. We weren't booked together. It just turned out that way. I was upset with the guys, because nobody showed up to make the rehearsal. Three of the guys didn't get to town in time, so we had to pull it together onstage. It would've been nice if they could've at least learned the songs. But my stuff is basically simple, so it worked."

"I was sitting at Atlantic mixing a record when, the next thing I knew, there's a package for me from Switzerland. They'd sent me the tapes of the performance," Joel recalled. "So I put them on—'Compared to What?' and 'Cold Duck Time.' The air-conditioning at Atlantic was broken at the time, and the doors to the studio were open, and the place just went nuts! If you wanna talk about what jazz is—jazz is a bunch of guys gettin' together and clickin' at the same time. It made the festival, and it made Les and Eddie into an act. Then everybody started to record at Montreux. It became the new Newport. The record [*Swiss Movement*] was a smash. It went from jazz to R&B to pop. Everybody was playin' it! In all the years I was at Atlantic, *Swiss Movement* was the only recording that Nesuhi and I coproduced, and the funny thing was that neither of us were at the performance," Dorn laughed.

"So Eddie got a manager, Marv Lagunoff, and Les got Peter Leeds," Joel continued. "Now the managers are fighting over whose name's on top, and they get into all this bullshit. They had a hit record, and everybody's actin' like fuckin' idiots. Les was much easier to get along with than Eddie. Eddie was a nice guy, a responsible guy, but he was ornery. He had a thing about success. He was into rehearsing. Eddie practiced day and night. He was a 'my way or the highway' guy, while Les just walks onstage and plays. He was like, we made this thing on the fly, let's just follow it. They were getting along. Then they weren't getting along. He and Les were incredible onstage together, but offstage there was no hookup. They were like the comedy team of Laurel and Costello."

"We really tried *not* to work together," Les joked. "His manager and my manager had major conflicts. Someone would book us. It seemed like a very simple thing to do, but then it always turned into a problem. Whose band were we gonna use, Eddie's band or my band? Why don't we use both bands together? Then there were money troubles. Who's gettin' paid what? I used to say, 'Fuck it, when it's right, I'll work with him.' We didn't do that many jobs together. The albums were more important [*Swiss Movement* and the 1971 follow-up, *Second Movement*].

"One of the breaking points was when his mother told him, 'That boy can sing! You should stick with McCann, 'cause he knows what he's doin'.' Now, we all grew up listening to Eddie, and she thought he ought to listen to me! So it was fucked on every level," Les laughed.

"Eddie was the human equivalent of a Rubik's Cube," Joel

imparted. "He would get a hit, and then he would do everything in the world to show everybody what he was about other than the hit. He didn't like to play his hits. He didn't want to be defined by them. He wrote books. He was into astrology. He was a one-of-a-kind guy, an absolutely brilliant musician."

"I've listened to Eddie Harris since I was a kid," Lenny said. "He was an amazingly technically accomplished saxophone player, much more than people really understand. If you're a player, you can tell he's got amazing chops. I went through all of his exercise books when I was younger. The technical exercises that he wrote for himself to practice were really challenging—excruciatingly difficult to play. He was a real innovator, but people don't always recognize it, because he did it in a way that was so acceptable by the public. At the same time, Eddie was an exotic. He did stuff like putting a mic on the strings of an electric bass but never plugging it in. He was not afraid of picking up an instrument with a classical history and playing it in his own style, ignoring whatever criticism might come his way for doing so, which is a beautiful thing. He just didn't care and was gonna do what was right for him and not worry about the criticism. Rahsaan Roland Kirk was similar. He was immune to criticism. That would never be an issue for those guys. This is not a time for people like that. We don't have many characters like that anymore."

"Eddie Harris was very stoic and very quiet," Atlantic Records' arranger and producer Arif Mardin recalled in a phone interview a week before his passing in June 2007. "He was very modern and inventive. He used a device called the Echoplex, which, at the time, was state of the art. It created the reverb on *Silver Cycles*. He'd play one line, and the machine would reply; so he would play these licks measuring how the machine would react with the repeats. It was beautiful. He also had a special mouthpiece so his tenor sounded like a trombone. I was so fortunate to work with him on his next to last musical project in the early '90s. It was called *Listen Here*, with the Köln orchestra [1992, Enja Records]. He was ill, but he still could participate."

Forever creative and driven, Eddie would eventually taper off his inventions and would choose to stick with his funky brand of bop until his death on November 5, 1996.

"I always wanted to play with Eddie. I was a huge fan of all his records and loved his work," guitarist John Scofield enthused. "Back in '93, I made a record called *Hand Jive* for Blue Note with my band [Larry Goldings, Dennis Irwin, and Bill Stewart] and Eddie as our special guest. He came to New York and recorded with us. One of the songs was dedicated to him. It's called 'Do Like Eddie,' and the solo he played is really phenomenal, one of his greatest recorded works. Then we toured with him, and he was really great. We learned a lot from him, all the guys in my band and me. Even though he had some big hits, I felt that he was neglected. At that time, acid jazz was getting big, and DJs were playing his hits, songs like 'Listen Here,' in discos; and everyone would dance to them, but nobody knew it was him. Eddie was completely unique. He could play the blues and soul music with this beautiful tone that was almost like Lester Young. He didn't have to scream, although he could. His intervallic playing was phenomenal. Eddie was very, very modern. He could play bebop, but he played the blues and soul music, and it was beautiful the way he combined it with modern jazz. That's why Miles loved him. He was goin' in the same direction at that time. He didn't play the Varitone with us. I would have liked it if he had, but he wasn't into it anymore by the '90s. He was just playing tenor, but he would do some amazing things. He would go through the history of jazz saxophone in a standard or over rhythm changes. He would run down Lester Young, Coleman Hawkins to Dexter Gordon, and Stan Getz to Coltrane and Sonny [Rollins]. He could imitate them all. Eddie was great to get along with, but sometimes he would want more money than anybody could give him. We would've had to give him all the money for the band and more. I understand why he felt that way. It was a response from having been ripped off in the past. He sold all those records with Vee-Jay, and maybe he didn't make the bread off that."

What can you expect from a cat who actually once titled an album *I Need Some Money*?

Back in 1978, Joel released a record called *A Tale of Two Cities* on his Night Records imprint of some rare live tapes that Eddie had stashed away in his garage. The album showcased Harris's diversity. "There was one track where he sang through his saxophone and sounded like Billie Holiday," Dorn reminisced. "On another, he plays 'Giant Steps' faster than Trane. And he did 'Chicago Serenade,' with that feel like he used on 'Exodus,' and a hundred other songs like 'The Shadow of Your Smile.' "

Whenever anybody talks about Eddie Harris, they in-

MAYBE HE THOUGHT HE WAS A BETTER MUSICIAN THAN EVERYONE ELSE AROUND HIM, 'CAUSE HE KNEW EXACTLY WHAT HE WAS DOIN'.

evitably talk about his trademark feel, a nonstop groove that wouldn't quit.

"I tell young people that I meet that it's one thing to play good, but, at some point, you gotta start playing the music. Most people don't ever go deep enough to bring it out. Most records don't have no feel," Les grumbled.

Ten years after their falling-out during the *Silver Cycles* sessions, Eddie and Joel had reached a detente. "We started talking and became pals again," Dorn said. "Then, the next thing I knew, he got sick. He got bone cancer. It was horrible…a horrible ending. The whole floor was full of banana peels for the last three or four months of his life. I recently went through cancer, so I know that cancer cures everything but cancer. [*laughs*] He became a different guy. I would talk with Yusef, Fathead, Hank, Rahsaan, all the guys, but Eddie was not part of that. He tended to be aloof, and even though he was a good guy, he had a way of turnin' people off.

"In one of our last conversations, he asked me, 'What is it about me that turns people off?' I said, 'You! You're such a great guy and a brilliant musician, but you got that attitude.' Eddie was a good pianist, so what he would do was, as people were leaving the room, he'd go over to the piano and do what Les just did. I don't think he was intentionally trying to be nasty, 'cause he was a funny guy, a good hang-out guy."

Les recalled, "He'd practice for six, seven, eight hours every day. Maybe he thought he was a better musician than everyone else around him, 'cause he knew exactly what he was doin'. He'd come off the set and be upset with me, 'cause what I played wasn't good enough. Then he'd go and do an hour or two by himself on the piano. After he did that a number of times, I just said no more. As crazy as he might be, that was the makeup of that human being which made him unique."

Being a "genius" is a lonely gig, especially when there are still plenty of people out there sleeping on the fact. Eddie had hits. He'd toured the world for forty years, and now his music was being sampled by a new generation that included Macy Gray, Jazzy Jeff and the Fresh Prince, and Heavy D. Eddie's obsession with perfection sometimes pushed him to doing things that came off rather cold. Not only did his showboating aggravate Les, but, at a moment's notice, he'd turn into a street fighter and shred the competition in a saxophone cutting contest.

"Right before he got sick, we were in Montreux for some anniversary concert for Atlantic," Dorn recalled. "Claude [Nobs] loves jam sessions. He had Eddie, Joshua Redman, and some other guys up onstage. Eddie was from Chicago, the capitol of the cutting session. In Chicago, you had Jug [Gene Ammons], Von Freeman, Johnny Griffin, Eddie, and a dozen guys you've never heard of. Jug would hand you your fuckin' head in a bag. He'd play 'Cherokee' in a key that didn't exist, at a tempo Jesse Owens couldn't catch. Guys would blow all they knew in a half a chorus, and their fingers would start bumpin' into each other. Joshua Redman is a good musician. He took four or five choruses. Then, in true Chicago tradition, Eddie blew everything Redman played in his first chorus. Then he played with his feet…his ear…he blew that joint apart. He handed the kid his head but not in a bad way. It was more like a right of passage. He was showing him how it was done in Chicago. It was like the guys who went to Kansas City in the late '30s and had the bad fortune of running into Lester Young or Basie's band."

"When he got sick, he became like a lamb, a totally different guy. He realized how difficult he was," McCann sighed, then paused a moment, and cleared his throat. He said earnestly, "Every musician I know who played with Eddie all speak about how deeply they were touched and what they learned from him. But, y'know, for all our differences, me and Eddie were actually both the same sign: Negro—penis rising," Les joked.

"Eddie also had a tendency to be a clown," Lenny said. "Perhaps it made people take him less seriously." Much to his fans' chagrin, Harris released an album of stand-up schtick in 1975 called *The Reason I'm Talkin' Shit*.

"Once you loosened up around him, all you did was laugh," Les recalled. "His wife, Sally, was like Gracie Allen, and he was George Burns. Eddie had a thing about who died that day or that week. He would let everyone know. We were all over in Europe touring with the band, and he said, 'Damn, like twenty-five saxophonists died this year!' And his wife said, 'Ain't you glad you're a drummer?' " ○

NEW FROM INNER CURRENT

PLUS ULTRA EP
TAKE
Off kilter future heaters remixes & collabos by Daedelus, Lukid, Domu & Ras G

IC009 -LP/Digital

BLESSED BY A YOUNG DEATH
GLEN PORTER
Sparse guitar phrasing & dark deconstructed breakbeats.

IC010 -CD/Digital

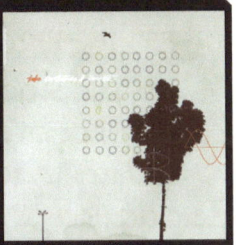

EARTHTONES & CONCRETE
TAKE
Take is foraging a brand of deeply listenable instrumental hip-hop. Hypnotic, psychedelic, laid-back, in other words, thoroughly West Coast." –Tomas Palermo, XLR8R

IC008 -2xLP/CD/Digital

GREEN TEA MINT
AKELLO UCHENNA
Introspective durrty south psych-hop, somewhere between Madlib & James Baldwin.

IC007 -CD/Digital

SECOND HAND MUSIC
MILFORD REYNOLDS
Dusty hip hop instrumentals via true school aesthetics.

IC006 -LP/Digital

INNER CURRENT RECORDINGS
Distributed by Crosstalk International
innercurrent.com | crosstalkchicago.com
myspace.com/innercurrent

AVAILABLE DIGITALLY THROUGH ITUNES, BEATPORT & EMUSIC

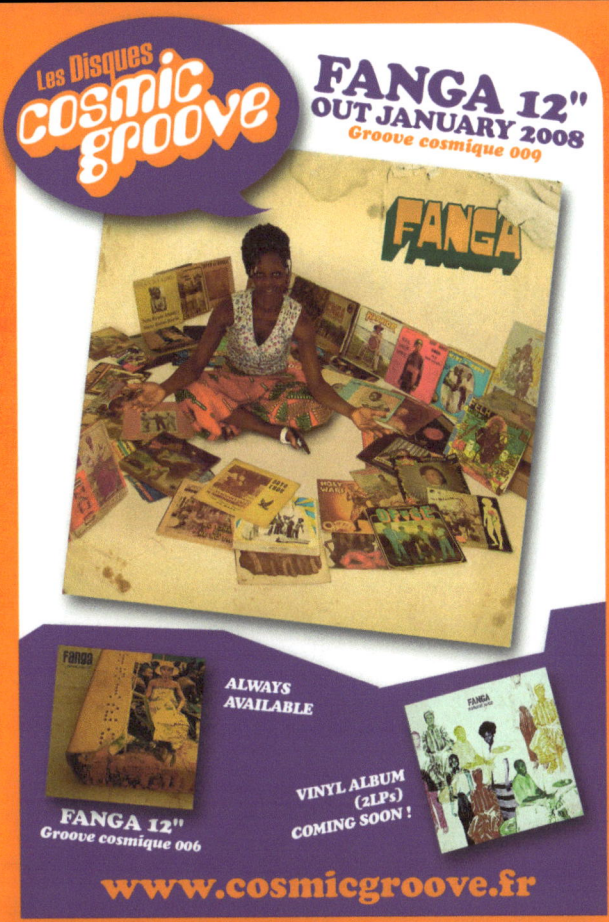

PS58 Available on Vinyl and CD

Joe Higgs' long out of print 1975 classic, remastered w/ original artwork and incisive liner notes

"Even a reggaephobe would have to concede: This one is a work of genius"
— Andy Perry/MOJO

www.pressure.co.uk

Definitive Jux Presents

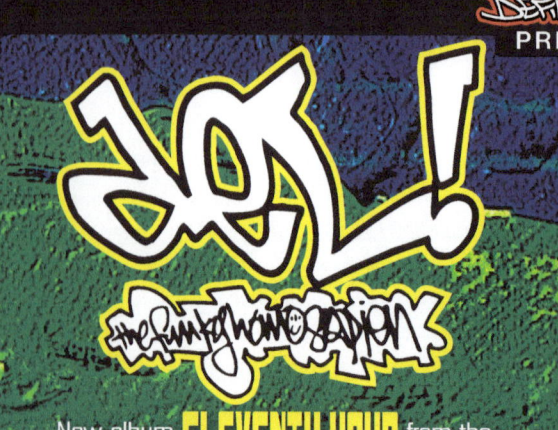

Del the Funky Homosapien
New album **ELEVENTH HOUR** from the man that brought you the classic albums:
I Wish My Brother George Was Here
No Need For Alarm · Deltron 3030
and the hit Gorillaz song "Clint Eastwood"

MYSPACE.COM/DELTHEFUNKYHOMOSAPIEN
AVAILABLE MARCH 11

definitivejux.net

Dizzee Rascal — Maths + English
THE NEW ALBUM — MATHS + ENGLISH HITS THE US WITH A PHYSICAL AND DIGITAL RELEASE CONTAINING NEW MATERIAL INCLUDING TWO NEW STUDIO TRACKS AND AN EL-P REMIX OF THE SINGLE "WHERE DA G'S" FEAT. UGK

WWW.DIZZEERASCAL.CO.UK
AVAILABLE APRIL 29

RECORD KICKS...NEW DEEP FUNK FROM MILANO

RKX019 CD/2LP/DIGI - OUT NOW
THE NEW MASTERSOUNDS RE::MIXED
NMS need little introduction to Deep Funk fans, at the forefront of the new funk scene since Keb Darge first booked them. Record Kicks have long been fans and came up with the idea of a remix collection. The result is a future classic, an absolutely essential compilation full of irresistible interpretations featuring Kenny Dope, Nostalgia77 & Corinne Bailey Rae, Smoove, Lanu ...
iTunes 2007 R&B/Soul best of 2007

RKX021 CD/LP/DIGI - OUT NOW
SOULSHAKER VOL. 4
"Funky soul galore -- all of it current, and all of it plenty darn great as well! Back when the first volume of this series was released, the idea of contemporary funk was a bit of a novelty -- but now, the deep funk underground is really getting some key exposure on a global level -- and a collection like this is a good reminder of why it's so great in the first place!"
Dusty Groove Chicago

RKX020 CD/LP/DIGI - AVAILABLE FROM 17 MARCH
BABY CHARLES
Described by Mojo Magazine as "an act to lead the 2008 soul uprising!" with 3 heavyweight 45s already under their belt, Baby Charles are finally back with the long awaited debut LP. Their fans include some of the world's top funk DJs including Snowboy, Keb Darge, Jazzman Gerald and Andy Smith, who snapped up their debut 45 for his "Let's Boogaloo! Vol 4" compilation.
100% deep funk from the new funkville Brighton!

RKX018 CD/LP - OUT NOW
LET'S BOOGALOO! VOL. 4
"Top draw collection of latin, funk and Northern Soul from the man behind the stellar Document Mix series and the DJ limb of Bristols genre defining Portishead in the 90s. Mr Smith takes the reigns for what is Vol. 4 of their Boogaloo series sewing together gems from the fields of funk Northern Soul and Latin Boogaloo. Big hitters old and new come from the likes of The Sweet Vandals Eddie Palmieri The New Mastersounds and Baby Charles"
Fat City

DIGITAL DOWNLOAD ONLY AVAILABLE FROM 28 JAN
UNITY BLANKS EP
Modern Soul for active listeners featuring Ernesto (Beanfield/Atjazz), Colonel Red (Bugz in the Attic/Domu) and Lizzy Parks (Nostalgia77).

RK45014 - 45 RPM/DIGI AVAILABLE FROM 11 FEB
BABY CHARLES
Storming Afro-Beat infected funk rework of the Arctic Monkeys' hit "I bet you look god good on the dancefloor"

RK45015 - 45 RPM/DIGI AVAILABLE FROM 11 FEB
DIPLOMATS OF SOLID SOUND + THE DIPLOMETTES
2 cuts from forthcoming Doss album featuring "Hurt me so" LACK OF AFRO rmx

---

SHOP ON LINE AT: www.recordkicks.com
recordkicks@recordkicks.com • www.myspace.com/recordkicks

Time taken for revelation = elevation time.

 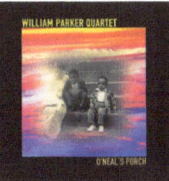 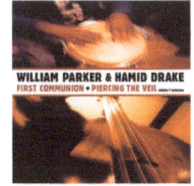  

>>> forward >>>

  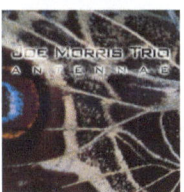 

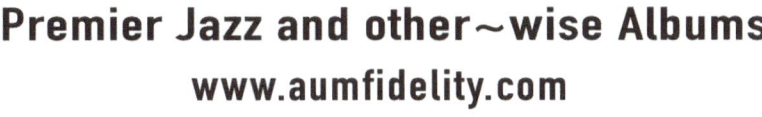

Premier Jazz and other~wise Albums
www.aumfidelity.com

---

dubspot

redefining music education

create.mix.record.produce

dbspot.com
877.dubspot
8 w 14th st nyc

learn to dj & vj
electronic music production
ableton.logic.protools.reason
courses.private events.youth program
open house sundays 12-2pm

© 2008 DUBSPOT. ALL RIGHTS RESERVED. ALL LOGOS AND TRADEMARKS ARE PROPERTY OF THEIR RESPECTIVE OWNERS

THE PINCH HITTER

Multi-instrumentalist Derf Reklaw holds a key position in the Chicago lineup

text
John Kruth

photography
B+

Derf Reklaw, the percussionist/multi-instrumentalist/vocalist formerly known as Fred Walker, has been employed as the secret weapon for Chicago-based jazz and funk musicians since the late '60s—including Eddie Harris, Ramsey Lewis, Donny Hathaway, and the AACM (Association for the Advancement of Creative Musicians). Derf has collaborated with Chaka Khan and Stanley Clarke, and was also a member of the legendary Pharaohs.

To describe him with words like "creative" and "inventive" only shows the weakness of our language. Not only does the man have a solid handle on the history of the music he has lived and breathed, he's a great storyteller and joke-smith as well, spewing one hilarious tale after the next in a mad ramble of jazzspeak.

When did you first meet Eddie Harris?
I first met Eddie in 1968. He was a guest soloist with the Operation Breadbasket band that was led by Ben Branch. We talked briefly about a few things. Then, in 1972, I was playing in a group with Eddie, Richard Muhal Abrams, Rufus Reid, and Billy James. In '73, I became permanent with him and played with Eddie until late 1974.

Being a multi-instrumentalist, what instrument did you mostly play in Eddie's band?
I didn't just play one instrument with Eddie. I played tablas, timbales, djembe, and conga drums. I also played flute and sang. And later on, I played saxophone too. I play all the saxophones, but when Eddie would play the reed trumpet, I'd go to the alto sax. That was a great band. I've played with several great musicians throughout the world, but Eddie Harris was the best. There was absolutely nothing that he couldn't do, whether it was yodeling or playing the piano. He was one of the best piano players I ever saw. He would take newspaper and put it inside, between the strings, and then he'd play the piano and it would sound like drums. I never saw anybody else do that. And he'd played saxophone with a trombone mouthpiece and trumpet with a saxophone mouthpiece, and later on he used a trumpet mouthpiece. Sometimes, he'd put bells on his fingers and just play the pads of the saxophone and hum through it with a wah-wah pedal and a phase shifter. Then he would sing through the saxophone like Billie Holiday.

When he was an MP in the service, he could take a gun away from somebody in three seconds. Whether it was playin' basketball or shootin' pool or crackin' jokes, he was the best. He could crack jokes for a whole set and be funny. He loved to embarrass you. If you were in your room at the hotel with a DO NOT DISTURB sign on your doorknob, he would take it down and write "Smokin' Herb," and then put it back on the doorknob! [*laughs*] Eddie was funny like that.

I used to practice the flute in my hotel room; so, one night in Montreal, Eddie invited me to play a solo for the people. The whole band left the stage, and I played a couple little songs that I wrote. People liked it, and he came back up and said, "That wasn't too bad. We'll see if you do the same thing the next set and repeat yourself," because he was the type of person that if you repeated yourself, he would write your whole solo out and hand it to you. He heard every note you played, and he could write it out. He said, "If you're gonna play the same thing, then you might as well read the music." [*laughs*]

But he was one of the few people I looked to as a mentor. He told me all kinds of things I needed to know to be a better musician, and I am a better musician from my association with him. Eddie would be playin' some of the baddest saxophone in the world, really fast, and then he'd would walk up on you and give you that look in his eye, to see if you could play as fast as he could. He liked to change things up. Sometimes, you'd play thirty-five songs on one night. Then, the next night, we'd play three. You never knew what was goin' on! He'd tell me to play the melody on the congas! He always had stuff to challenge you and trick you with. With Eddie, the whole thing was to play beyond the bar line. I started yodeling and he out-yodeled me. He could play the drums like Max Roach. There wasn't nothin' he couldn't do.

So then why did you leave Eddie for Ramsey's band?
Well, Eddie was *real* thrifty, and I had kids and a wife and bills. After he moved to Los Angeles in October of '74, I knew he wasn't gonna be flyin' me back and forth from Chicago to wherever he had to play. So I wound up playin' with Ramsey after that. He made me an offer I couldn't refuse. You got your clothes, hotel, and a per diem. Charles Stepney, who I did a lot of work with, told me, "Eddie is never gonna forgive you for leavin' his band."

I had to tell Eddie that I was leavin' 'cause I was gonna get my own band together. I knew he'd understand that. I couldn't tell him I was leavin' to play with Ramsey. He said, "Well, okay, but I was gonna make you a star." I said, "Huh?" Eddie never made nobody a star. Then, one of the first jobs I had playin' with Ramsey, Eddie and Donald Byrd were also on the show. Some friends came backstage and asked Eddie, "Derf's not playin' with you?" He said, "No, Derf is with Ramsey. We can play without Derf, but Ramsey needs all the help he can get!" [*laughs*] I wrote a song called "Get On Down" that Eddie had a little hit with. Then he went on *Soul Train* doin' the moves that I had choreographed for the band. They were up there doin' my song and my moves, and it was funny, 'cause I wasn't nowhere in sight.

Didn't you used to play in the Pharaohs?
Yeah, the Pharaohs, as a collective unit, was the best group I ever worked with. They had all the potential in the world but blew it. When I joined in 1968, I was asked by "Ki" [Charles Handy], who was the leader of the Pharaohs.

Some of that stuff was really out there, approaching Sun Ra's dimension.
Very few of the real Pharaoh songs ever got recorded. Of the two records that were released by Ubiquity, only two of those songs made the Pharaohs famous. We recorded some songs at a studio in Chicago that nobody's found—the masters just disappeared. We had one song that I wrote with Chaka Khan singing before she was famous. That's over forty years now! [*laughs*] Unless you saw them live, the world never really heard the real true Pharaoh music. It's funny, everybody's makin' a big thing about the Pharaohs now, but where were they when we were performing? They never saw us.

What was it like working with Donny Hathaway?
When I first met Donny, he was the happiest person on earth. We were really good friends, and he'd show me stuff he was comin' up with at his studio on 77th and Halstead. I worked with him on several projects, like *Come Back Charleston Blue*, and we did some Afro Sheen commercials. I worked with him when [conga player] Master Henry [Gibson] couldn't make it. But Donny was a brilliant arranger and great singer and a funky piano player. When he did "The Ghetto," he didn't know it was gonna hit. When it did, he wasn't used to bein' in the public life. Bein' a star messed him up a little bit, and he didn't recover from that.

Did you cut anything with Donny on Atlantic?
No, but I recorded with Eddie on Atlantic—*Bad Luck Is All I Have* and *I Need Some Money*, which I wrote [the title track for].

Comin' from Chicago, you were in with the AACM—Association for the Advancement of Creative Musicians, started by Muhal Richard Abrams in 1965.
Yeah, I played with Muhal Abrams's AACM Big Band with Roscoe Mitchell and Anthony Braxton, Joseph Jarman, Lester Bowie, and Malachi Favors. When I saw Joseph Jarman, he was playing the things that I'd been thinking about playing. I first played flute, oboe, and clarinet, and became a drummer after my instrument got stolen. I never had a teacher. I taught myself how to play drums in two weeks, and then I formed my own band.

So what are you up to these days?
Freelancin' on various projects 'round town, doin' soundtracks. I played some music with Stanley Clarke, and I'm on staff at various universities and colleges, doin' dance classes at UCLA. ●

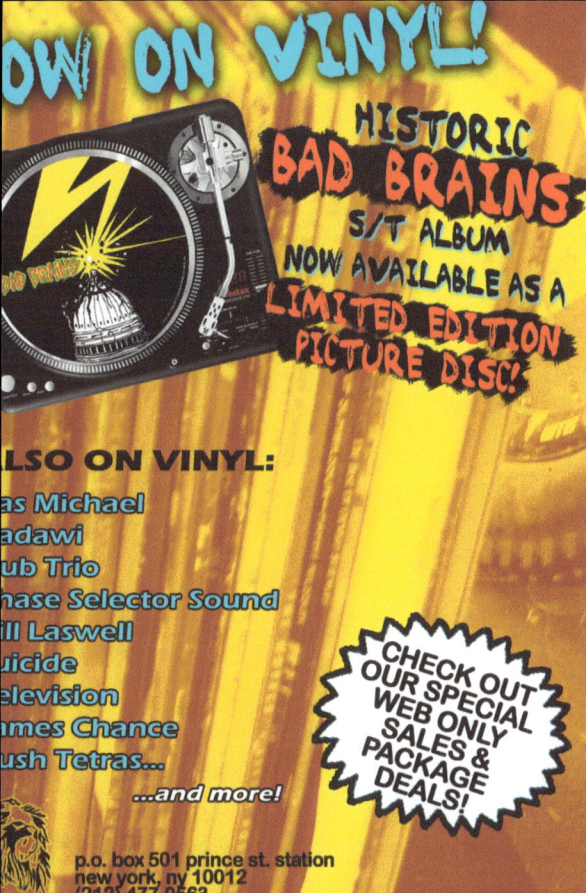

NOW ON VINYL!

HISTORIC BAD BRAINS S/T ALBUM NOW AVAILABLE AS A LIMITED EDITION PICTURE DISC!

ALSO ON VINYL:
as Michael
adawi
ub Trio
hase Selector Sound
ill Laswell
uicide
elevision
ames Chance
ush Tetras...
...and more!

CHECK OUT OUR SPECIAL WEB ONLY SALES & PACKAGE DEALS!

p.o. box 501 prince st. station
new york, ny 10012
(212) 477-0563
catalog@roir-usa.com
www.roir-usa.com

BOBBY WILLIAMS FUNKY SUPER FLY
Explodes Across The Nation Like The Atom Bomb

THIS ALBUM CONTAINS HIS GREATEST HITS
LET'S JAM - FUNKY SUPERFLY - LET'S WORK A WHILE ...AND MORE!

New from **Jazzman**, the very best of deep funk legend **Bobby Williams**. Available on compact disc and triple vinyl 7" with extensive liner notes and previously un-seen photos, featuring his greatest hits **Let's Jam, Let's Work A While, Funky Superfly** and many more.

Coming soon:
7" **Bill Swift Trio** Chain Of Fools
CD & 2LP **Various Artists** California Funk

worldwide mail order from
JAZZMAN WE DIG DEEPER
www.jazzmanrecords.co.uk

Tru Thoughts recordings

Quantic Soul Orchestra
Tropidélico

This album has already been heavily supported by the likes of Bobbito, Gilles Peterson and Mr Scruff. Pushing the funk sound forward for the 21st Century.

"Funk is the driving force... what's not to love?" **XLR8R (USA)**

"Assembled across several continents whilst skillyfully blending the players different inclanations" **The Independent (UK)**

"Drenching jazz with Latin sunshine" **BBC Music Magazine**

"A cracking listen" **Cool Hunting**

Hot 8 Brass Band
Rock With The Hot 8

"Awesome. Nothing quite like it. One of the summer's essential tunes!" **BBC 6 Music**

"Funk, jazz, skank, hip-hop and stonking Dixie blue. A solid gold album of the year contender. 5 STARS*****" **New Zealand Herald**

"Stands head and shoulders above many of its current contemporaries" **DJ Mag**

"Magnificent. You've never heard anything quite like this before" **One Week to Live**

"It's classic, you've got to hear it to feel it, feel it to believe it." **Soul Riot Magazine**

| Quantic & Nickodemus feat. Tempo & The Candela Allstars 'Mi Swing Es Tropical' 7" | Nostalgia 77 'Quiet Dawn' 12" (Includes Bonobo & Povo Mixes) | Hot 8 Brass Band 'What's My Name? (Rock With The Hot 8)' 12" | Saravah Soul 'Nao Posso Te Levar A Serio' 7" | The Bamboos 'I Don't Wanna Stop' 12" (feat Kylie Auldist) |

21st January | 28th January | 11th February | 18th February | 3rd March

Visit **www.tru-thoughts.co.uk** for all tour dates, releases and news, and listen to our radio shows anytime on **www.totallyradio.com**
All Tru Thoughts & Zebra Traffic music is available direct from **www.etchshop.co.uk**

DIGITAL CHEMISTRY

Newcleus is at the center of the electro cosmos

text
Adam Windmill

photography
Cozmo D

In the early 1980s, hip-hop was going through a change. With advancements in electronic music-making technology too tempting to resist, a few pioneering artists started experimenting with drum machines, synthesizers, and sequencers to create an electronic hip-hop sound. Electronic music wasn't new, but electronic hip-hop was. Newcleus, with their trademark spacemen-with-attitude approach, funky atmospheric bass lines, and wikki-wikki scratch, played a big part in this change. Newcleus gave us a taste of the future, and, although not alone, they played a major part in introducing the world to electronic funk.

The futuristic qualities of their music, along with their humor, gave them an appeal that reached far greater than their native New York. Not only did they achieve Top 40 *Billboard* successes at home with their first two singles, "Jam On Revenge" and "Jam On It," but they also influenced a whole generation of future music makers.

Battling in Brooklyn throughout the '70s, Cozmo D, the founding member of Newcleus, was at the spearhead of the growth of hip-hop there, yet he had a message he wanted to take to an even bigger place. Through his music, he wanted to change the world.

Is it true that the originally titled "Jam-On's Revenge" only made it onto your demo because you had space to fill at the end of the tape?
Cozmo D: That's true! At the time, the four of us—myself, Bob "Chilly B" Crafton, Yvette "Lady E" Cenac, and Monique "Nique D" Crafton—were going by the name Positive Messenger. We were all deeply Christian, although in a much more spiritual than religious sense. We had gone on a mission of making music with a message. All of our songs were either about Christ, our spiritual beliefs, or about human and world conditions.

Of course, I was also DJing with my crew, Jam-On Productions. We'd been rockin' the streets and parks in Brooklyn from the very early days of hip-hop but weren't really feeling the majority of rap records released to that point; this was about '81. One of my fellow DJs, Salvadore Smooth, kept nagging me about why we didn't do any rap records. Finally, I decided to have some fun with Sal—instead of making a rap song, I made an anti-rap one ["Jam-On's Revenge"].

So, by this point, you'd already been together for quite some time. How was Jam-On Productions originally formed?
Well, the roots of Jam-On actually began with myself and my two first cousins, Nique and her little brother, Pete "Master Quadro" Angevin. In the spring of '75, I'd been inspired by hearing a tape of a Coney Island DJ called Count JC—he'd been rocking the bass break to "Bra" by Cymande. From that point on, DJing was what I wanted to do. At high school, a couple of my friends had a little DJ system, and I would hang out with them at their crib. Sometimes, my cousins would come with me, and they caught the bug too. Eventually, we got our own little system and started DJing together in '76.

When Nique left for college the following year, we got my long-term best friend, Dave "Dr. Freeze" St. Louis, to take her place. He'd been DJing with another long-term friend of ours, Al "T" McLaran—they'd been using the name Jam Brothers Incorporated. To make Freeze feel like an equal, we took on the name Jam-On Productions.

Nique got back from college and started going out with Chilly B, who, at that time, had his own DJ thing going on. That was also when I met Yvette—she joined as Lady E [later to become Cozmo's wife]. At our largest point, we had six DJs and ten MCs. Our core, though, was always myself, Quadro, Freeze, MC Harmony, Nique D, Lady E, Master J, and DJ Kane.

In 1983, "Jam-On's Revenge" caught the attention of Joe Webb at May Hew Records and was released as a 12-inch. Later that year, it was also released by Sunnyview Records. During this time, "Jam-On's Revenge" by Positive Messenger turned into "Jam On Revenge (The Wikki-Wikki Song)" by Newcleus. Could you talk me through these changes?
Now *this* is a long story!

In 1980, with a cheap synthesizer and drum machine, I started trying to make my own music. I got Jam-On together, and we did a rap song called "Freak-City Rappin'." Naturally, I thought it was a hit and set out on my first deal-shopping mission. None of the companies I visited would even listen to it until I went to Reflection Records. Only one person worked there—a guy by the name of Joe Webb. He listened to the tape, gave me some constructive criticism, and encouraged me to keep working at it. Soon afterwards, I borrowed enough money from Nique to purchase a Tascam Portastudio [one of

Newcleus

(from left) Paul "Fresh Kid" Webb (dancer), Denise "Neicey D" Roberts (backup singer), "Tracy G" Green (drummer), "Nikki D" Crafton (singer, keys), Bob "Chilly B" Crafton (keys, singer, bass, rap), Yvette "Lady E" Cenal (vocals, keys), Ben "Cozmo D" Cenal (vocals, keys), Hector "Slam" Rios (dancer), Otis "Lil' O Me" Brown (dancer), circa 1984.

the first multitrack cassette recorders]. She asked, in return, that I did some music with Bob Crafton [Chilly B]. Right from the start, musically, we went together like a hand and glove. Positive Messenger was born.

Two years later, right after we had recorded "Computer Age," I felt we had a hit on our hands, and I was ready to try shopping for a deal again. I also felt I owed Joe Webb for being the only person who'd given me a shot earlier. It turned out that Reflection Records had folded. I checked to see if his name was in the phone book, and, sure enough, it was. I called him, and he invited me over to his house—he really dug "Computer Age," but when "Jam-On's Revenge" came on, he practically lost his mind!

We didn't want to release "Jam-On's Revenge" as Positive Messenger; the song was almost a betrayal of our mission. We wanted a good name that would depict our makeup as a group. We all lived together in the same house—it was almost like we were one family unit. Monique and I were first cousins—she was married to Bob, and I to Yvette. As the group represented the nucleus of three different families, Nucleus seemed like the perfect name. Joe Webb told us some crap about scientific integrity, so we changed the spelling to Newcleus.

Webb released it on his own label, May Hew Records—the title at that point was still the same, but a mistake by whoever did the label's copy listed the song as "Jam-On Revenge."

Jonathan Fearing, a club DJ that would spin on the weekends at WBLS, was the first to jump on the record. Soon it was making lots of noise in the city, and Joe Webb did a deal for it with Sunnyview Records. They brought in Fearing to edit the song so it would have an arrangement similar to the one he played on the radio. Sunnyview then released it—somehow in that rerelease they lost the hyphen between "Jam" and "On." It's been known as "Jam On Revenge" ever since.

After the success of "Jam On Revenge," you decided on "Jam On It" as your follow-up single. Was that an easy choice?

The plan was for "Computer Age" to be our second single, but, following the success of "Jam On Revenge," Sunnyview requested we did a rap record instead. At first, we were resistant, but, as we'd already compromised with "Jam On Revenge," we figured we'd go ahead and give the label what they wanted. I threw together a funky beat, adapted a bunch of rhymes from Jam-On's park-rocking days, came up with a hook, and "Jam On It" was born.

"Jam On It" was huge, and Sunnyview said it was time we did an album. When I say huge, I mean huge. Everywhere we went, the record was on fire. It was crazy! We'd go from town to town and turn on the radio—"Jam On It" was always on. We had no intentions of being a rap group, you know. A lot of the stuff I wanted to put on the album [*Jam On Revenge*], I didn't; the record company only wanted dance music.

"Where's the Beat" was a song that didn't seem to fit with the rest of the album.

"Where's the Beat" wasn't our song! At the time, that stupid Wendy's commercial with that old lady going "Where's the beef" was a big commercial. Joe Webb was like, "Hey, you guys need to do a record called 'Where's the Beat.'" Now, I like having fun, but I don't like corny, and I didn't want to do a stupid record. He got these guys, Dennis and Dave Williams, to do it. Webb finally talked me into laughing at the end. To this day, I regret even doing that; it gives it a sense of legitimacy it doesn't deserve.

You believed Joe Webb was looking after your interests?

Yeah, that's the truth. Even though we weren't making any money, he kept saying, "Oh, we're in the red, we're in the red." I had a huge-ass record—I was touring and performing in front of thousands and thousands of people. I knew something must have been happening right.

Jonathan Fearing was mixing all your music. Why was he given so much control?

He was the first to pick up our record when it was still on May Hew—so he actually broke the record. They rewarded him by saying his touch is gold and gave him everything. The next thing we knew, he had complete control of our music—once it got in his hands.

So you were being shut out musically by Fearing and financially by Webb?

Right! In our case, [Joe Webb] came at us with some contracts. I asked if I should take it to a lawyer; he said, "Nah, I'll explain it to you." We signed, and never saw the contracts

Cozmo D and Chilly B (in dark blue) in the studio.

again. We didn't get any royalties—still haven't! We did get paid on the road, but Webb probably took most of that money. They paid the dancers as much as they paid us. He was taxing us this way, that way. [*laughs*] He was getting us good!

I've read that "Why" was one of your favorite Positive Messenger songs, but you didn't want it to go on an album.
We didn't put "Why" on the first album because it didn't fit: that was my decision. When MIDI came out, which was after the first album, I wanted to test it out; "Why" was the first thing I worked on. Joe Webb had a silent partner called Frank Fair—I think he put the bug in Joe's ear for us to put "Why" on the second album. I wouldn't have put it on: first, because it didn't fit, again, and, second, because now I'd seen what Fearing was doing to our songs. Joe just kept working on me and working on me. At first, I said no, but we had some room to fill; there were a couple of songs [Sunnyview] wouldn't let in. One was called "Get Looser." I want to find a copy of that so much! Like "Jam On It," "Get Looser" was something we did completely raw. It was like a wikki-wikki thing about us taking over a radio station and making fun of rap records. Sure, I'm biased, but I really feel "Get Looser" was five times the record "Jam On Revenge" was!

So Joe Webb is still working on me for "Why." Eventually, I said okay, but under the condition that Fearing doesn't touch it. "I give you my word, Ben," Joe said to me. Sure enough, sure enough, shoot! Fearing had just come out of hospital and was too sick to go to the studio. He made Sunnyview put equipment in his apartment—he mixed "Why" there.

Sunnyview gave Fearing "Why" to mix right after he'd come out of hospital, even though he was still too ill to work in the studio?
That's right, and you can hear it! He's much better than that! You know when you listen to "Why" that something was wrong. He went right back from there, right back into hospital and died. It's sad; I don't wish that on anybody!

Towards the end, we were so disgusted. We realized we were getting ripped off and felt so helpless that we cut ourselves off.

How did you make your move into producing?
[Sunnyview owners] Adam Levy and Henry Stone said to us,

Chilly B in the studio.

Chilly B and Niqué D's sons, Justin and Jason, with Cozmo D and son BJ. Christmas 1984.

"You can't go out and be Newcleus, but you can go out and produce." That was an outlet for us—what we wanted to do was music. Of course, we would rather perform it ourselves, but if our way to be free was to produce for other people, then that was great! The first track we produced was "Greedy Girls." We did it on Sunnyview so people would know that it was Newcleus, but with other guys rapping. It got a nice write-up in *Billboard*, and everything was getting ready to happen. Recollection fails me, but it felt like only weeks after the record was released that Sunnyview went under. I always loved that track! It definitely told us we can do this: we can produce—we never looked back.

Joe Webb formed a new Newcleus and continued to put out records. Did his Newcleus still tour and perform your songs?
They would occasionally do a show here and there—every now and then I talk to Mike Skinner, who was in the original phony Newcleus; he told me Webb had this planned all along. Almost immediately after we left, he put them in the studio.

Nique D and Chilly B split up. Did that cause any conflict?
Yeah, when their whole thing went sour, it was pretty deep. A lot of personal things happened—things that had been hidden over the years came to the fore. When they split up, we split up.

Was that the end of Positive Messenger?
Newcleus was really the end of Positive Messenger. Our time and our energy went away from the positive and more towards making dance records, but that was definitely the end of Newcleus right there. It wasn't until Rhino Records approached us in '97 that we thought about being Newcleus again.

Rhino Records wanted to put together a best of Newcleus album?
Yeah, and they needed help. They also asked us if we could come up with a new Newcleus song. We did "Jam On This (Old School's Back in Session)." It was the first time we'd got back together in ten years.

It wasn't until this whole revival thing started happening that I realized so many people still held on to our music. I felt I needed an online presence, so [I] put up jamonproductions.com. I started recreating the records—I wanted to put them out the way we originally did them. We put them all together to make an album, Destination Earth—which I've started selling over the Net. I'm not getting rich; matter of fact, I'm just paying my bills, but I'm paying my bills doing what I love most in this world. ⊙

For more info on Newcleus, visit jamonproductions.com.

WINTER MUSIC CONFERENCE
MARCH 25-29, 2008
MIAMI BEACH, FLORIDA

2ND ANNUAL WMC
RECORD COLLECTORS SHOW

Saturday, March 29, 2008
12pm - 6pm
Miami Beach Resort & Spa
4833 Collins Ave, Miami Beach

- LP's 12"s, 45's, 7"s, cassettes, and memorabilia
- All genres!!!
- Listening stations provided for testing/reviewing
- Battery operated turntables allowed
- Reputable dealers
- No bootleg may be bought or sold at the show

waxpoetics

   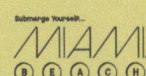  

 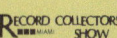

3450 NE 12th Terrace • Fort Lauderdale, FL 33334 • Phone: (954) 563-4444 • Fax: (954) 563-1599
Website: www.WinterMusicConference.com • Email: info@wintermusicconference.com

NYPH 08

New York
Photo Festival
May 14–18

Curated by
Martin Parr
Lesley A. Martin
Tim Barber
Kathy Ryan

The Future of Contemporary Photography

Information: +1 212 604 9074
newyorkphotofestival.com

  VII

BOOMBOX DISTRIBUTION NETWORK

SPECIALIST DISTRIBUTION OF INDEPENDENT SOUL, FUNK, JAZZ, BEATS, HIP HOP etc.

NEW RELEASES:

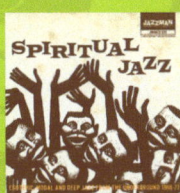

SPIRITUAL JAZZ
VARIOUS
(JAZZMAN CD/LP)

CONNIE PRICE & THE KEYSTONES
TELL ME SOMETHING
(UBIQUITY CD/LP)

GHOST
THIS IS WHAT MY SOUL LOOKS LIKE
(BREAKIN' BREAD MIX CD)

MILLION DAN/DEMON BOYZ
SCREAM OUT b/w GLIMITY GLAMITY
(MILLION DAPPA)

ERIC LAU
NEW TERRITORIES
(UBIQUITY CD/LP)

FUNKSHONE
DROPPIN'
(SKYLINE 7")

BESTSELLING BACK CATALOGUE:

NICOLE WILLIS & THE SOUL INVESTIGATORS
KEEP REACHIN' UP
(ABOVE THE CLOUDS REISSUE CD/TIMMION LP/MP3)

BREAKIN BREAD
DIRTYBEATBREAKINFUNKANDHIPHOP
(BREAKIN BREAD CD/EP/MP3)

COLOR CLIMAX
PLUG IT IN
(BREAKIN' BREAD CD/MP3/12")

DJ CASH MONEY
HEADBANGIN' FUNK 45's
(BDN MIX CD)

DEMON BOYZ
RECOGNITION
(SUSPECT-PACKAGES REISSUE CD/12")

LEWIS PARKER
MIXTAPE VOLUME ONE
(THE WORLD OF DUSTY VINYL CD)

FOR MORE INFO, PROMOS, PRICING ETC CONTACT:
WWW.BOOMBOXDISTRIBUTION.NET INFO@BOOMBOXDISTRIBUTION.NET

ONCE UPON A TIME IN THE BOOGIE DOWN BRONX

Grandmaster Flash and the Furious Five help hip-hop get props

text Mark McCord

It was a historic night for music history. For hip-hop, it was the last barrier of mainstream acceptability. The creators of rap music were going to be recognized by the same institution that honored rock icons Chuck Berry, Little Richard, Bruce Springsteen, the Rolling Stones, and Ray Charles. The Rock and Roll Hall of Fame induction ceremony takes place every year at the posh Waldorf-Astoria Hotel in New York City; for music history buffs as well as old rock fans with salt-and-pepper hair, this is the night. Music critics and record industry heavyweights turn out in droves to celebrate the careers of the rock legends that inspired the music we all know and love.

But the 2007 award ceremony was different. This was the first year that a rap group would be inducted into the hall of fame. Rock fans and music critics were livid. Twenty-seven years after "Rapper's Delight" shook the world, the genre still wasn't respected as a legitimate form of music. "I've heard of Grandmaster Flash," scoffed one irate fan online, "but who in the hell are the Furious Five? And why on earth are they being inducted into the Rock and Roll Hall of Fame ahead of INXS?"

Last year, the group that practically invented rap as we now know it was formally inducted into the 2007 Rock and Roll Hall of Fame, alongside rock greats R.E.M., Patti Smith, Van Halen, and the Ronettes. This is a large step for a crew that many have called the greatest rap group to ever grace the stage or wax. Their story starts in 1976, when it really was just about the music.

Grandmaster Flash
photography Lisa Haun/Michael Ochs Archives/Getty Images

THE GENETIC CODE

Back in 2005, on a warm day in Oakland, California, I had the opportunity to sit and interview the man who wrote the genetic code for what we call hip-hop today: Kool DJ Herc. But back in Herc's day, it didn't have a name; it was what it was: just a neighborhood thing.

After listening to the founding father reminisce about his times as the first breakbeat DJ progenitor, I realized something: Kool Herc is to hip-hop what Alexander Graham Bell is to the telephone. Yes, he is the creator. But what hip-hop was then and what it is now are two different things.

One hundred years ago, you couldn't have paid Bell or an Italian gentleman named Guglielmo Marconi to have predicted the wireless phone, the cell phone, the BlackBerry, or any other modern device. Kool Herc himself will tell you in a heartbeat, "I had no idea that this would become a billion-dollar-a-year industry."

With that in mind, I wondered something: if Coke La Rock (Kool Herc's MC) was just spittin' little phrases on the mic, not all-out rhymes as we know it today, then who was the first real MC spittin' lyric for lyric, on beat, with a continuous flow?

"Mr. Herc," I asked him as I scratched my head and searched for the right words, "I'm curious about something. Who was the first person that you saw rap as we know it today?"

At that moment, a warm smile enveloped Kool Herc's street-hardened face. He looked out the window and across the street at Lake Merritt, almost as if he was looking back at that day, and, in a quiet voice, he said, "It was Melle Mel—Melle Mel and Kid Creole. They were at a boxing gym on 169th Street, in the Fort Apache area; as a matter of fact, it was the last place that I seen Big Pun alive at."

In a quiet and almost somber voice, he recalled the events, sometimes taking a pause to look down at his battle-scarred hands: "They was in the middle of a boxing ring with these big Afros. Kid Creole, as little as he is, had one too. Flash was behind them cuttin'. When I saw them, I just smiled, 'cause I knew where they got it from. They got it from me. And they knew that they got it from me. I wasn't mad. Melle Mel saw me in the crowd and just nodded at me. I laughed to myself."

It must've been one hell of a moment.

Hanging above the dimly lit gym was a thick cloud of smoke, a pungent mixture of cigarettes and reefer laced with angel dust. Stoned dust heads tripped out as the dazzling display of flashing lights played psychedelic tricks on their minds. In the red-light haze, surrounded by stick-up kids, gangsters, and hyperactive b-boys, Kool Herc got to see the first steps of his creation taking on a new dimension, as brothers Melle Mel and Creole were laying down the foundation for rap as we know it today.

According to Kool Herc's suddenly upbeat, mocking recollection, "They were saying, 'Yes, yes, y'all, to the beat, y'all, a keep on, y'all, and ya don't stop.' "

Mel and Creole—born Melvin and Danny Glover—are from the South Bronx, an area that was once described as a war zone. It was here where they were born and raised—them and six other gentlemen who would fill out the group Grandmaster Flash and the Furious Five. The group's rise from hip-hop pioneers to 2007 Rock and Roll Hall of Fame inductees was long and hard. Their story starts in the grimy streets of the South Bronx, where they were all fans of an amazingly innovative local DJ.

GRANDMASTER CRUSHES THE COMPETITION

"This group has never been just about five people," Arthur "Disco Bee" Hayward says to me while looking out his window and smoking a cigarette. What he is referring to is the fact that, apart from the five MCs (Melle Mel, Scorpio, Rahiem, Creole, and the late Keith "Cowboy" Wiggins) and the DJ, Grandmaster Flash, there were actually two other guys who were a part of the crew, Flash's assistants: Disco Bee and EZ Mike. "I go back with him to the beginning," Bee says. "You ask around, anyone that knows the truth will tell you that originally it was Grandmaster Flash, Disco Bee, and the Three MCs."

On this day, Bee is a bit frustrated. The impact of the band's induction into the Rock and Roll Hall of Fame could finally turn the page for a group that many mainstream media outlets have ignored over the last twenty years, thus generating some serious cash for a generation of aging hip-hoppers who never got the chance to see any real revenue for the music they've given most of their lives to. Further adding to the situation is that the contributions of Disco Bee and EZ Mike have practically gone unacknowledged. "Flash didn't invent any of this by himself!" Bee says to me. "That shit [a three-man turntable routine] that he did onstage at the VH1 Hip Hop Honors with Jazzy Jeff and Kid Capri is the same thing that me, him, and Mike did back in the day."

Disco Bee goes back to Flash's initial stages at a schoolyard called 63 Park. Bee, as friends like to call him, would be there with another young man named Cordee-O, whose older brother was Flash's partner, "Mean Gene" Livingston.

Disco Bee at Disco Fever
photo courtesy of Disco Bee

Disco Bee, along with Flash's best friend, EZ Mike, helped Flash innovate the turntable tricks that would elevate him from the status of local DJ to turntable god.

Today, Disco Bee is a middle-aged man living in North Carolina with his family. With his Bronx accent, glasses, and trademark baseball cap, Bee still retains much of the flavor of his Boogie Down Bronx upbringing. He is rather subdued while talking about his beginnings as a teenaged DJ more than thirty years back, but immediately snaps to life when the subject switches to his favorite sound system. "The Gladiator!" he exclaims with an exaggerated, raspy voice, while proudly wrinkling his face into an intimidating sneer, stretching out his arms, and bringing them together as if he was wielding a mighty sword. This was the system that enabled the group to compete with some of the most ground-shaking sound systems in the tristate area.

In search of further clarification on the power of the Gladiator, I ask EZ Mike, Flash's best friend since childhood, about it.

"What?" Mike says, as his deep, death-like, gravelly voice hits a high pitch. "What? No one could touch that system. It was untouchable. When we started playing the Dixie, this guy on Freeman Street, this Jamaican guy, built this thing for us."

Beaming with pride thirty years later, Disco Bee recalls, "The speakers were as big as refrigerators, and we had four of them. It took two people to carry the amp, this was so fuckin' heavy. We used to put a towel over it, so while we were carrying it into the club, people would be pointing at us wondering what we were carrying. And then…we'd uncover it. They would be blown away by…the Gladiator!"

Bee and his partner EZ Mike went all around the city destroying other crews in sound clashes. That was until one night in Jamaica, Queens. "We were at this club on Hillside Avenue," remembers EZ Mike. "The Fantasia, that was it. There we were with the Gladiator; Flash was killing them people. He was cuttin' that record 'Catch the Groove' to pieces: *Dunna dunna dun.* [*imitating the sound the sax squeal makes as it's sliced and diced to pieces*] *Dun-dun-dun-dun-dun-dun-dun-dunna dunna dun. Dunna dunna dun.* He was killin' it. He was spinnin' around and shit like that, cuttin' the record…and then, all of a sudden, we heard this huge, monstrous sound go *DUNNA DUNNA DUN.* Flash snatched the headphones off and looked around at us and said, 'What the fuck was that?' We had no idea what it was, but it was so loud and clear that he could hear it even through the headphones! So he went back to spinnin' again. I happened to look across the room when I saw [Michael] Goode, in a wheelchair, push a button on his mixer, and then we heard it again: *DUNNA DUNNA DUN.* We were all like, 'Oh shit, that's their fuckin' system making all of that noise.' They fuckin' drowned us out; even with the Gladiator, they fuckin' drowned us." That was the night they met DJ Divine and Michael Goode and first witnessed the awesome power of their set called the Infinity Machine.

But, still, Flash and his gravity-defying, lightning-quick turntable techniques made him a very difficult DJ to defeat back then. "One day after Flash had beaten Herc and all of them, there was a jam at a park," EZ Mike tells me as his voice becomes louder as he gets more excited. "Herc was playing there. From the moment we got there, people were like, 'Yo, there goes Flash.' This nigga did one of the most awesome things I had ever seen in my life. He got on the turntables and started cuttin' 'Good Times.' He was killin' that shit: '*Good…good…good…good times…good times…good times. Good times. Good times.*' And he kept doin' it faster and faster: '*Good times, good times, good times.*' Motherfuckers were watching this shit and were buggin' the fuck out. And then, all of a sudden, he stopped and walked away from the set. He just kept on walking past the ropes—we thought he was done. And then, all of a sudden, he went running back toward the turntables at top speed and flipped the cross fader just in time for the record to go: '*Good times.*' I swear everybody in the fuckin' park lost their minds."

The rep was growing. Flash was the DJ equivalent of a mighty god like Zeus or Apollo. But he couldn't conquer the city alone.

THE KING OF THE STREET

Formerly a self-professed crack addict, now a muscle-bound, tough-talkin', protein-shake-drinkin', rumored-to-be sometime male stripper, and aspiring wrestler called "Muscle Simmons," Melvin Glover is known as one of the greatest rappers to ever touch a mic: Grandmaster Melle Mel. That the first real "King of Rap" sometimes moonlights as a male exotic dancer is heartbreaking to hear. You see, for many rappers of a previous generation, Melle Mel was the equivalent of the mystic Bob Marley and the hard-partying funk god Rick James. For many, Melle Mel was like a prophet. Just like no one would've wanted to see or hear about Bob Marley or Martin Luther King Jr. shaking their stuff onstage wearing nothing but a thong, no old-school hip-hopper wants to hear about—or, more importantly, wants to see—the great Melle Mel dancing somewhere in a thong as part of the "Gun Show."

I have my doubts as to whether Mel is really an exotic dancer or not. So I ask him point-blank: "Mel, I hear this whole 'Gun Show' thing and you being a stripper is just an

extension of a joke that you and Scorp' started some years back." To which he responds: "I do my thing. I'm not gonna comment on that. I got my hustle."

Just like I thought.

Today, at forty-five years of age, Melle Mel is not ready to hang his mic up or coast his way into oblivion. In fact, he's probably more over the top today than when he was in his prime. He's probably one of the few rappers alive these days who actually walks it like he talks it. He's a man's man in a culture that doesn't value maturity. Anyone lacking in self-confidence could borrow a cup or two from him, or, at the very least, could take notes. Even when he's at his most boastful, he's being sincere. "I made a way for me to do what I do and for them [other rappers] to do what they do. When you see Melle Mel, I want people to know that you're seeing a true-to-life living Black legend," he says to me with the raging confidence of a wrestling legend like Ric Flair. When he's not in the gym or onstage dancing in some club, he's touring the country promoting his first solo album titled *Muscles*.

In the late '70s, Mel was known on the streets as "Flash's MC." He was the central voice for the baddest DJ the world had ever known at that time. In many ways, they complemented each other: Mel was at the very pinnacle at what he did, and Flash was unstoppable. It hadn't always been the case that Mel was the best MC, though. Many people, who remember them from their days as the Three MCs, recall when Mel's older brother, Danny (aka Creole), was the best of the trio. In typical fashion, Mel tells me quite confidently, "That's subjective, who was better than who. Creole was good, but he wasn't better than me."

In the Morrisonia section of the Bronx where they grew up, there were many fledgling MCs that got on the mic for Flash in 1976. In fact, according to Mel, "Anyone could get on the mic for Flash back then." Lovebug Starski has made claims of being the first person to talk on the mic while Flash was cutting. But it is the late Keith Cowboy that many remember as being Flash's first real MC.

While Cowboy, Lovebug Starski, and others were doing their thing with Flash in the park, the Glover brothers were hard at work preparing to take their neighborhood by storm. "Me and Creole were in the house every day practicing and polishing our routines," says Mel. "From the very beginning, we did everything together. We used to listen to Kool Herc and them. They used to say things like, 'And yes, y'all, the sound that you hear...' They were always saying 'and yes, y'all.' We really liked that, so we used it. So we would take that and lengthen it, and say it to the beat. So it would be, 'A yes, yes, y'all, to the beat, y'all, freak, freak, y'all.' We went to all of Herc's parties and studied their shit," he continues. "We studied their format just like people would later study us; that's how we studied Herc. There are a bunch of stories out there that say that Creole got on first, and I got on a month or something like that later; no, we got on the mic for Flash at the same time."

From the very first time that Mel saw Coke La Rock and Timmy Tim on the mic, he says that rhyming became an all-consuming obsession for him. "I knew from that very first time I held the mic that this is what I should be doing," he tells me. He said as much on his very first record, "Superrappin' ":

Ever since I talked at my very first party,
I felt I could make myself somebody.
It was somethin' in my heart from the very start,
I could see myself at the top of the charts,
Rappin' on the mic, making cold, cold cash,
With a jock spinnin' for me called DJ Flash.
Signing autographs, for the young and old,
Wearing big-time silver and solid gold.
My name on the radio,
And in the magazines.
My picture on a TV screen.

No one would've guessed back then that all of that would come to pass. It can be argued that Mel's competitiveness, ego, and raw determination were key ingredients in putting the band at the top of the heap. Everyone interviewed for this article agrees that Mel was far more competitive than the rest of the group. To this day, he believes that not only can he body slam any opponent in a wrestling ring but can still defeat any MC out there as well.

Many rappers over the age of thirty-five consistently cite Melle Mel as a prime influence. Rappers as diverse as Kid 'N Play, Big Daddy Kane, Hammer, Busta Rhymes, Too Short, Rakim, and Kool G Rap have all praised his name over the past two and a half decades. His lyrical prowess is unmatched with songs like "World War III," "Step Off," "Beat Street Breakdown," "King of the Street," "New York, New York," "The Truth," and "Survival." He stood out in an exceptionally talented group.

Nowadays, it's a hard task to get the band that changed rap music to reunite. So much has happened over the years: drug abuse, breakups, fights over money, lawsuits, envy, bitter feelings for not being properly credited, and death. But before the group was full of animosity, before the records and movies, Grammy Awards, world tours, long nights with strings of groupies, and critical ac-

Mr. Broadway, Kid Creole, Rahiem, and Lavon—Grandmaster Flash's post–Furious Five band who signed to Elektra after Melle Mel parted ways in 1983
photography **Raymond Boyd/Michael Ochs Archives/Getty Images**

claim, in his heart, Melle Mel was Flash's biggest fan.

"Ladies and gentlemen, the sound that you hear is a def to your ear. Ya have no fear, 'cause Flash is here. The disco dream of the mean machine, the Darth Vader of the slide fader, no man in the world cuts straighter or greater than New York's number-one cut creator." That's how Melle Mel would open many a show with Flash back in the day.

"He's the one that made me wanna get in the game," Busy Bee tells me of Melle Mel. Busy is one of the group's biggest fans and himself a hip-hop pioneer who is best known for his appearance in the movie *Wild Style* and his record *Suicide*. He remembers how the guy that he was so much a fan of was possibly an even bigger fan of Grandmaster Flash: "I used to see him walk around in a sky-blue T-shirt that said 'Pro Keds.' Now on the bottom of the logo that said 'Pro Keds,' he wrote 'Flash fan.' He was a Flash fan. And he wore the shirt so much that that's the way I knew who he was. It was sky blue with white letters; I'll never forget it. I still have snapshots to this day of Mel in that shirt. [Like] what Monique [the comedian] said to the Bishop Don 'Magic' Juan: 'If you wear that green suit again motherfucker!' You know what I'm sayin'? 'If you wear that T-shirt one more time, motherfucker, I'll buy you a joint my motherfuckin' self.'"

EZ Mike remembers when Mel first came around their crew to get on the mic: "Mel wanted to get on the mic with Flash, because [Flash] was the best. It was Flash that put him on. Mel and all of them followed Flash everywhere. They were fans of the man just like everyone else."

Whether it was on tape or on record, Mel was usually the lead voice. With an almost fire-and-brimstone delivery, he'd convey lines about Flash so convincingly that people thought that it was Flash on the mic: "Grandmaster Flash is willing and able; he's the king of the cuts on two turntables. He's the grand grand, the master man. He's so nice on the slice, he don't need no band. He rocks 45s and 33s; he rocks boys, men, women, and young ladies!"

THE SVENGALI

Not many people today remember Sylvia Robinson as a singer. She is probably one of the first Black females to find success as a songwriter and producer. But, without a doubt, the biggest feather in her cap is that she is the first Black female recording artist to own her own independent record company. Many people call her a genius. There isn't a thing about record production that Sylvia Robinson doesn't know. On a recent rerun of the syndicated show *Soul Train*, a flashback segment highlighted old footage of Sylvia from 1973. "And now from the *Soul Train* history book, this is Sylvia," Don Cornelius said as he introduced her with his trademark smooth-as-velvet bass voice. The camera cut to a scene from the distant past, where a dance floor full of teenagers with Afros and bell-bottoms swayed to the sultry sounds of an erotic disco beat. Onstage wearing an oversized jazzy yellow applejack cap and big hoop earrings, Sylvia Robinson moaned and whispered between sensually charged verses: "What your friends all say is fine, but it can't compete with this pillow talk of mine."

And to think she almost sold the song to Al Green. In 1973, the song "Pillow Talk" was not only a top-ten smash hit on the radio, but it was also a hit in discos, bedrooms, and in the backseats of cars parked in dark places all over America. The song "Pillow Talk" resurrected a career that dated back to the 1950s when Sylvia, as part of the R&B duo Mickey and Sylvia, burst onto the charts with the smash song "Love Is Strange."

Along the way, she wrote and produced for Bo Diddley, Ike and Tina Turner, the Moments, Shirley and Company, the Whatnauts, Brother to Brother, and many others. Sylvia knew a hit when she heard one. Whether it was the Moments singing the R&B classic "Love on a Two Way Street" or Brother to Brother covering Gil Scott-Heron's "The Bottle," the lady knew her stuff. To top things off, she and her husband, Joe Robinson, a tough, no nonsense, gruff kind of guy, made the ultimate coup d'etat in the record biz in 1975 by buying the Chess/Checker catalog.

Or so they thought.

By purchasing the Chess/Checker publishing catalog—a collection of some of the most treasured songs in early rhythm and blues and rock and roll history—the Robinsons invited the jealous wrath of White record men. They gave Joe and Sylvia pure hell from the moment they bought that catalog. "Niggas weren't thinking about buying publishing catalogs back then," a defiant Joey Robinson Jr.—son of the couple—tells me on the phone.

In 1979, their record company, All Platinum Records, was struggling financially. That was until Sylvia saw Lovebug Starski performing at the club Harlem World; that's when a light went off: "What if I could take what he's doing and put it on wax?" After thirty years in the music business, Sylvia knew to trust her instincts. It would be those instincts that had helped her to navigate the treacherous waters of the music industry for three decades that wouldn't allow her to let the idea go. First, she approached Lovebug Starski, who turned her down. According to DJ Hollywood, the man that many credit as being the "godfather of rap," she approached him as well, and he too turned her down: "I was making so much money at the time playing at the Apollo and Club 371 and other spots around the city that making a record didn't make sense to me at the time." That's when she got the three guys from New Jersey and christened them the Sugar Hill Gang and released the first commercially successful rap record, "Rapper's Delight." The Robinson's label was the first independent record company in the world to rake in serious cash from a brand-new style of music, which, much like rock and roll, would later have a profound impact on popular culture.

LEGENDS IN LEATHER

By 1981, Sylvia Robinson's choke hold on the rap industry was complete. She signed all of the top groups in the city to contracts—ironclad contracts, at that—so that no one could compete with her stable of acts. The best crew on her roster was Grandmaster Flash and the Furious Five. They were the real kings of rap back then. And they were an arrogant bunch, too.

Cold Crush Brothers' DJ Toney Tone remembers a night at the early hip-hop hot spot the Disco Fever, when Scorpio "spent all night looking at himself in the mirror." Many groups from that time remember the Furious Five as being the types of guys who were a little too full of themselves. Kool Herc remembers Melle Mel as being one of the only ones who would occasionally come out and play with him and his crew. As brilliant as they were, their competition at that time would've been shocked to learn that the band only practiced "maybe once a week," according to Rahiem. "We didn't really practice that much, because Mel and Creole didn't get along. Every time we would get together, it never failed, they'd get into it, and one of them, usually Creole, would wind up walking out. We *may* have practiced one day a week, but it was *intense*; we practiced from three or four o'clock in the afternoon to ten or eleven at night."

Today, at forty-three years old, Rahiem is the youngest member of the crew and arguably the most talented. His smooth tenor voice and wicked flow made him the lyrical coanchor of the band. Whereas Mel is boastful and arrogant, in contrast, Ra is quiet and introspective. "People see me on the street and say, 'Hey, aren't you…somebody I should know?' They don't know if I'm from the Cold Crush or the Treacherous Three or what," Rahiem tells me. "I'm not as easily recognizable as everyone else, and I kind of like it that way." It was Rahiem who cowrote many of the group's songs along with Melle Mel.

Scorpio aka Mr. Ness was the ladies' man. It was his charismatic persona—with his braided hair and sharp features—that helped to give the quintet its swagger. Kid Creole, to this

Grandmaster Flash at Disco Fever
photo courtesy of Sal Abbatiello

day, still has long, flowing, straight hair, as well as nonstop rhymes, and a voice like a traveling salesman. But it is the late, bowlegged, deep-voiced Keith Cowboy who many revere. He had one of the best voices ever heard on a mic.

The most superb example of Cowboy at his best is at the end of the record "Freedom." As the tape was fading out, there were more rhymes to go, so the founding member of the Furious Five ended the song in a classic street-corner style with finger snaps and all. He wasn't the best lyricist in the group, but it was his voice and flow that forever sealed the ending of the song as a classic.

Once they got on Sugar Hill and their records started selling, they went way over the top as far as egos went. And why not? They toured the country with some of the biggest acts of the '80s: Evelyn "Champagne" King, the Gap Band, Joan Jett, the Clash, the S.O.S. Band, and many others. The band was royalty on the street. In Hollywood, they hung out and partied with Eddie Murphy. Their stage show was in demand. Night after night, they toured the world like proselytizers of a new faith. They were spreading the word of the gospel that Kool Herc had crafted ten years before and were taking it to places as unexpected as Aruba. People in Middle America had never seen or dreamed that eight guys with two turntables and a set of microphones could do so much with so little. They were warmly received in most places, but in others they were met with stone silence and indifference. What they were doing was so much different from anything anyone had ever witnessed.

"We were playing at Bond's International one night. I'll never forget this," Rahiem says as he recalls the show. "When we first started touring with Sugar Hill, Sylvia used to dress us. She picked out these velvet suits with rhinestones—we hated those suits. Anyway, here we are at Bond's International, opening for the punk rock group the Clash. Those White boys that came out [to hear the Clash], you know, they wanted to slam dance and shit like that. So Flash is out there first, doing his thing, and I guess he went *zigga zigga* one too many times, and the crowd started getting restless. Well, we get out there and start doing our thing, and, after a while, I dunno… It seemed like everybody went to take a break and head for the concession stand—at the same time. The next thing we knew, we were getting hit with all kinds of shit. I remember somebody threw an orange at Scorpio, and it hit him dead in the balls. It was that bad. And we had to go through it twice, because we played two shows that night. But we got over it, because we were being paid $18,500 that night. When we got off that stage, every White boy in that place looked like someone who threw something at us."

Bad shows aside, what making records afforded the group was the chance to tour the world. Some of them had never been outside of New York before; they were in awe of the sights and sounds of different places and having fans in neighborhoods that were similar to their own. "I'll never forget this time on tour in St. Thomas," says Disco Bee. "Me and Cowboy were the only ones who woke up early; it was eight o'clock in the morning, and everyone else was asleep. Cowboy said, 'Yo Bee, let's go out.' We were like two little kids with a new invention. I mean, we were that happy. We were walking around when, all of a sudden, we turned a corner and were like, 'Oh snap, you see that?' It was a bunch of brothers playing ball in a park with no shoes on. We joined in with them. After a while, Cowboy looked at me and said, 'Yo Bee, you gonna take your shoes off?' I said, 'Hell no.' He said, 'Me either.' The ground was too fuckin' hot for that shit."

"We really liked touring the country," Rahiem says. "One of the things that separated us from a lot of these cats today is we didn't just know our hood, we were in every hood," Melle Mel says adamantly. "A lot of these dudes today are block niggas, because all they know is their block. But when we came to town, we went into every hood and hung out and got to know the people." Rahiem agrees: "As soon as we'd get off the plane, we'd be like, 'All right, take us to get some food,' and we went straight to the hood. In every country and every city, we didn't care where, we went to the hood. We loved going to Florida. Atlanta was a good city for us, and we loved hanging out there. All over Louisiana—New Orleans, Lake Charles, Shreveport—we got plenty of love there."

"What did you love about Louisiana?" I ask.

"The food, the women. Once you've had a Creole woman—I dunno, man, that shit was like crack; that shit was addictive."

THE FURIOUS FIVE MEET THE KING OF PUNK FUNK

In 1982, Grandmaster Flash and the Furious Five sat on top of the rap music industry like a big 800-ton elephant. But the world of funk was the dominion of a shit-talkin', weed-smokin', cocaine-sniffin', sex-crazed, multitalented singer, songwriter, and producer named Rick James.

Decked out in leather and high-heel boots, James had only two real friends: a spliff and a guitar. With recordings like "Mary Jane," "Bustin' Out," "Standing on the Top," "Cold Blooded," and "Give it to Me Baby," Rick James was the king of funk. His songs weren't just about sex and drugs, though they were a common theme. He also liked to write tunes that reflected his ghetto upbringing: "P.I.M.P. the S.I.M.P." was a song he recorded with the Furious Five for the album *Cold Blooded*. His albums went platinum, and he played to sold-out stadiums all over the world. People who knew him have said that he was one of the hardest-working musicians they had ever met. For as hard as he worked, though, he partied even harder.

"People need to go back in their memory banks and remember, in the '70s and '80s, before Prince and Michael Jackson, Rick James was hot," Melle Mel wants to remind us. "He was the first modern-day Black rock star. When he walked out onstage and said, 'Fire it up,' everybody in the place was firing their weed up. He was a talented dude." Mel cites the song "Déjà Vu," which James wrote and produced for Teena Marie, as being his favorite Rick James record. "Slick Rick [as James was sometimes called] was basically like our father when we were out on the road," Mel tells me. "Slick Rick did for Grandmaster Flash and the Furious Five what Frank Sinatra did for Sammy Davis Jr. He made everyone respect us.

"When we first went out on tour with him," Mel continues, "we'd be outside our tour bus lifting our little weights that were filled with sand and doing push-ups. Outside the coliseum, or wherever we were doing a show at, we would get this little deli tray that would have meats and cheese and shit like that on it that looked like niggas probably could've wiped their balls with it. Rick would come around and check up on us and make sure we were all right. And he saw how we were being treated. He went to Al Hayman, who at one time was the biggest promoter in the country, and put him and the union people on notice: 'Yo, treat them right. Flash and them are my boys.' And they did it. So as a result of that, we got better food, better places to stay, more space onstage, and more time onstage."

"We immediately clicked with Rick," Rahiem tells me. "Although he's from Buffalo, he's still from New York. His drummer, Lino, from the Stone City Band, is from the Bronx—we all immediately hit it off. We got high together and everything."

"Did you ever hear Rick James say, 'I'm Rick James, bitch!'?" I ask.

"Absolutely!" Rahiem responds. "That was his slogan; that's really not a joke. That's how he really carried himself. I seen him straight-up kick a chick in the ass with a pair of thigh-high suede boots on. He was wearing some black leather pants. He straight-up kicked a chick, straight up her ass. He said, 'You must have the game fucked up; I'm Rick James, bitch! Get out of my dressing room.'"

Upon hearing Rahiem's story, Melle Mel laughs and remembers another event: "The first time I saw Rick, I hadn't even met him yet. I seen him smack the shit out of a bitch, and this was a good-looking broad too; I mean, he wasn't no punk about his. He smacked her and said, 'Now get the fuck out of my dressing room!' I was like, 'Oh shit, this nigga is for real.'"

Rick's charismatic personality and talent made a serious impression on the Furious Five. But there is another memory of Rick that really stands out for Mel: "When we would be onstage, Rick would be on the side of the stage wearing a hood over his head, watching us, silently taking mental notes. He really wanted to help us to be better performers."

Rahiem recalls a night after the tour was over, when "Rick called me when he knew he was going to be in New York, and told me to meet him at NBC studios on the set of *Saturday Night Live*, because he wanted to surprise Eddie. It was Smokey Robinson's birthday; it was me, Rick, Smokey Robinson, Jamie Lee Curtis, Eddie Murphy, and a lot of others who all went out to Studio 54."

"What was Studio 54 like?" I ask.

"The only way I know how to describe Studio 54 to you would be to say…it was like Disco Fever to the tenth power."

A MESSAGE IN THE MUSIC

While the group was out on tour having the time of their lives, Sylvia Robinson was excited about a demo she got from percussionist and songwriter Ed Fletcher—aka Duke Bootee. According to a 2004 article in *Blender* magazine, Fletcher had two songs on the demo; one was called "Dumb Love" and the other was "The Message." In the article, Melle Mel said, "No one wanted to do 'The Message'; even Ed Fletcher didn't think much of it."

At the time, the band was coming off a string of records that blasted out of boom boxes and rocked block parties, skating rinks, cookouts, and school dances—but they weren't hits. Saleswise, they were nothing in comparison with what was to come. "Freedom," "The Birthday Party," "It's Nasty," "Flash to the Beat," "Superrappin'," and "The Adventures of Flash on the Wheels of Steel" were top-notch rap records, but they didn't make it to the top of the charts.

The first commercial rap artist to release a record with any kind of social awareness was a guy who at one time had been a part of Flash's crew. According to Disco Bee, "At one point, the group got really large. I mean, there were a whole lot of people in the group, man." So they ended up having two groups: the A group, which was the Furious Five, and the B group, which consisted of Kool Kyle, Lovebug Starski, a guy named Georgie George, and another guy, who called himself Kurtis Blow.

According to the band, at first, no one in the group wanted anything to do with "The Message." It was a complete departure from everything that they had done. For a year, the band ducked and dodged Sylvia at every turn. But the more they resisted, the more pressure she applied. Finally, she put her foot down: either record this song, or that's it. "She'd do things like withhold advances from us as a form of punishment," Rahiem recalls.

According to Joey Robinson Jr., the reason Melle Mel is the only one from the group featured on the song is because Mel said, "Mrs. Robinson, if you believe in the song—then I believe in you." No one else in the band believed in the record.

Grandmaster Flash has gone on record as saying he was against the idea of only one person from the group being featured on the song. However, Rahiem was originally on the track as well. "Mel and I cowrote the verse 'a child is born' together; it was used on 'Superrappin',' says Rahiem. "We decided while recording 'The Message' that that part would fit into the new song." But then the script got flipped on Rahiem: "I laid down the part that Duke Bootee would later do. But Mrs. Rob had a problem with my mother and I. She called us troublemakers." From the very start of their careers at Sugar Hill Records, Rahiem's mother had a deep distrust for Sylvia Robinson. The bad blood mostly stemmed from the fact that Sylvia forced the band into signing the contract on the spot without legal advice. Rahiem says that he and his mother openly questioned Sylvia's controlling methods, which is why his voice was erased from the final track.

Every group has its standout member; whether it's the Leaders of the New School, the Wailers, or the Spinners, there is that one member who has a little bit more of that special *something* that makes that member stand out from everyone else. From the very start of their careers at Sugar Hill, Sylvia noticed that special *something* in Melle Mel. "It was Mrs. Robinson that singled him out and made it look like he was the leader—but he wasn't," Rahiem tells me. "Because his lyrics were more universal, we let him take the lead on stuff that he wrote."

In the song "The Message," Duke Bootee and Melle Mel painted raw lyrical pictures of the suffering of ghetto dwellers huddled together in the ruins of the neglected promise of America. For the first time on wax since the days of the Last Poets and Gil Scott-Heron, there was a record on the radio that truly captured the claustrophobic desperation and despair of the inner city at the dawn of Reaganomics:

Broken glass everywhere,
People pissin' on the stairs,
You know they just don't care.
I can't take the smell,
Can't take the noise,
I got no money to move out,
I guess I got no choice.
Rats in the front room,
Roaches in the back,
Junkies in the alley with a baseball bat.
I tried to get away, but I couldn't get far,
'Cause a man with a tow truck repossessed my car.

And then the song's refrain:

Don't push me, 'cause I'm close to the edge,
I'm tryin' not to lose my head.

When "The Message" finally dropped, it was one of the most awesome songs ever heard in rap up to that point. Lyrically, it forever changed the game. The days of party rhymes and fun were over. The seeds for a more serious art form were finally taking root. ⬤

KINDRED SPIRITS

SOUL PURPOSE IS TO MOVE YOU

NOW AVAILABLE WORLDWIDE

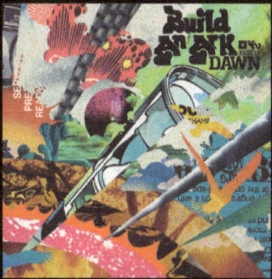

BUILD AN ARK
Dawn
Spiritual Folk Jazz. Recorded with underground legends such as Big Black, Dwight Trible, Phil Ranelin and others...

out on CD / 2xLP / Downloads

HAL SINGER & JEF GILSON
Soul Of Africa
1st time reissue of the '74 holy grail of french spiritual modern jazz with Jef Gilson on CD.

Also available : special Jef Gilson 10".

out on CD / LP / Downloads

MIA DOI TODD
GEA
Former Columbia-Jazz artist. Beautiful elevating guitar play, harmonics, vocals and string arrangements... A true folk gem!
Also available : Mia Doi Todd 7"

out on CD / LP / Downloads

REDNOSE DISTRIKT
POES
21 track album feat: Harco Pront, Mocky, Benny Sings, Melodee, Deborah Jordan (Sillouette Brown) and more...

out on CD / 2xLP / Downloads

ALL THINGS KINDRED
www.kindred-spirits.nl
myspace.com/kindredspiritsrecords

AKROBATIK
ABSOLUTE VALUE

fat beats records

THE LONG-AWAITED NEW ALBUM FROM THE MEMBER OF THE PERCEPTIONISTS.

BEATS AND GUEST VOCALS FROM TALIB KWELI, J DILLA, LITTLE BROTHER, MR. LIF, 9TH WONDER, ILLMIND, B-REAL (CYPRESS HILL), J-ZONE, FREDDIE FOXXX, DA BEATMINERZ AND MORE

IN STORES & ONLINE FEBRUARY 19
WWW.FATBEATS.COM   WWW.MYSPACE.COM/THEREALAKROBATIK

TORAE
DAILY CONVERSATION CD

DEBUT FROM BROOKLYN MC INCLUDES BEATS FROM DJ PREMIER, BLACK MILK, 9TH WONDER, MARCO POLO, KHRYSIS & MORE

ILL INSANITY
GROUND XERO CD & LP

ROB SWIFT OF THE X-ECUTIONERS LEADS A NEW GROUP THAT RAISES THE BAR FOR TURNTABLIST COMPOSITION.

FAT RAY & BLACK MILK
THE SET UP CD & LP

DETROIT PHENOMS FAT RAY AND BLACK MILK JOIN FORCES TO SET UP THE WORLD FOR A MOTOR CITY TAKEOVER IN 2008.

TRUTH & SOUL PRESENTS
FALLIN OFF THE REEL V.2 CD & 2XLP

BROOKLYN-BASED FUNK LABEL TRUTH & SOUL BRING ALL OF THEIR SMASH VINYL RELEASES TO CD FOR THE FIRST TIME. FEATURES RAEKWON, EL MICHELS AFFAIR, AND MORE

AVAILABLE EXCLUSIVELY FROM FAT BEATS DISTRIBUTION
110 BRIDGE ST   BROOKLYN, NY 11201   718.875.8191 PHONE   718.875.9297 FAX   DISTRIBUTION@FATBEATS.COM

THE FINEST SELECTION OF NEW AND CLASSIC HIP HOP ON CD & VINYL

FAT BEATS.COM / NYC / L.A.
THE LAST STOP FOR HIP HOP

Events | News | Music | Photos | DJ Top 5
Podcasts/Radio | Vimby Video | Imeem Playlist

...A. | NYC | ATLANTA | CHICAGO | DC/B'MORE | DETROIT | TORONTO
... AREA | NEW ORLEANS | BOSTON | HOUSTON | DALLAS | CHARLOTTE

...xt: PHILADELPHIA, COLUMBUS, MIAMI (WMC EVENTS) + MONTREAL

...EE EVENT UPLOADS for Progressive Music & Cultural Events | Seemless
...Operation on Mobile & PDA Devices | Easy Event Search | RSS Feeds
... Music Player + New Event Blogs + Much More... | Be In The Know!

www.fusicology.com

...gn up for our weekly event blasts @ www.fusicology.com

 # Timmion
RECORDS – WEB SHOP

LP'S
Nicole Willis & The Soul Investigators "Keep Reachin Up"
Nicole Willis "Sings...If This Aint Love"
The Soul Investigators "Home Cooking"
Didier's Sound Spectrum "TR-78"

45'S
NEW 45 OUT! The Soul Investigators "Pretty Women"
UPCOMING new 45 By The Soul Investigators Band!
Nicole Willis "If This AIn't Love"
Nicole Willis "Feeling Free"
Nicole Willis "Holding On"
+Others...

www.timmion.com

The breakthrough second LP from California's cinematic-soul brothers and backing band for *Big Daddy Kane, Brand Nubian, Slick Rick,* and *Too $hort*.

"Connie Price and the Keystones are to be praised for their originality and brilliance."
-Lalo Schifrin

"Connie Price has the "Key" to success and a sound that's solid as "Stone."
-Big Daddy Kane

((•)) Ubiquity
www.ubiquityrecords.com

THE WASHINGTON MONUMENT

Chuck Brown grounded go-go in the call-and-response of Chocolate City

text Thomas Sayers Ellis

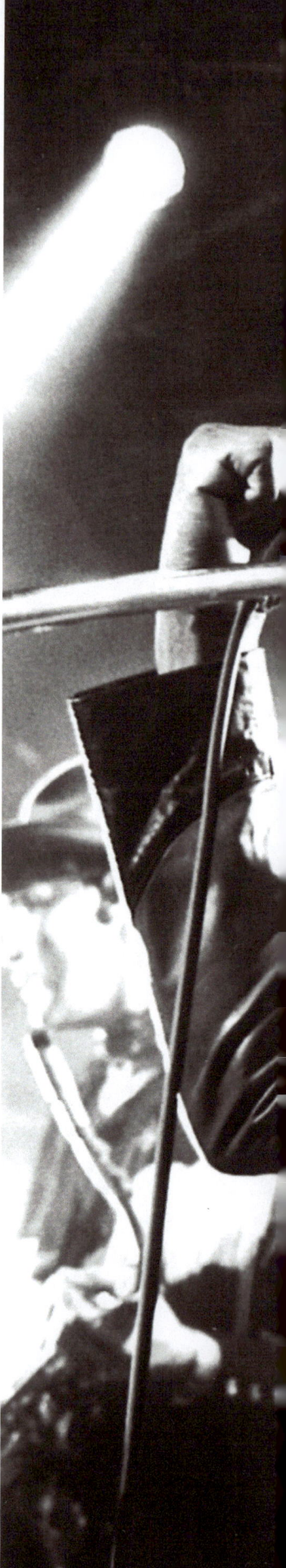

In Washington, D.C., there's a riot and a renaissance going on as the release of Chuck Brown's *We're About the Business* has reignited, across age and taste differences, that live-music-town feeling that took a historic and inward genre turn when Chuck Brown and the Soul Searchers, in search of a way to keep dancers on the floor between songs, began bridging grooves together with talk and percussive pockets. The now classic "Bustin' Loose" from 1978, with its chant against anti-liberation complacency and genre behavior, was the first result of that bold move, and ever since its release, go-go and its much-loved local architect have both kept going. Unlike hip-hop (whose muscular sampling is mostly studio fueled), go-go finds its strength in live performance, in the communal exchanges between the lead talker and area audiences, which include local crews. The line from Chuck Brown to the more original and successful inheritors of his style, such as the early Rare Essence and today's Backyard Band, is potholed with more bands, performances, and personalities than anyone can remember. But one thing is certain: Washington, D.C., is Chuck Town, and Chuck Brown is the most well-known and liked person inside the Beltway. A walk through D.C. with Chuck is like being on tour or on the campaign trail, and his legendary status has now been lifted by former go-goer and hot-handed producer Chuck Thompson. Together they prove that nothing keeps going (beneath song) like go-go, and that no one keeps going like Chuck, who continues to serve as a tough, honest, ambassador/parent to the wild child he created more than thirty years ago. With all-school flava and groove-deep, percussive Mafioso pockets, Chuck baby is back, full of blocks of party-rolling, hot-chopped barbecue and give-a-fuck.

Early go-go has a lot of organ, tambourine, and talk in it. What did you hear growing up, and where are you from?
I was born in Gaston, North Carolina, on August 22, 1935. I'm a Virgo, and when I was about six months old, my mother took me to Charlotte, North Carolina. She had a live-in job, and she worked there for a while. Then we moved to Emporia, Virginia, where she met my stepfather. Then we moved to Stony Creek, Virginia, from there to Jared, Virginia, Mechanicsville, McKinley, and Alberta, Virginia. I was the only child by my mother. I have several brothers and sisters on my real father's side. There are about twelve of us, and, all these years, I haven't gotten to know any of them. My father's name was Albert Moody, and he died when I was about six months old. My real last name is Moody, but I kept my mother's maiden name, Brown. So when we got to Richmond, Virginia, I went to Neighbor Hills School. I'd always been interested in music, and when I was about seven years old, I started fooling around a little with church piano. My mother kept me in church, and she used to stay on me about playing church music, strictly gospel; but by the time I was thirteen years old, I'd strayed, met a little girl, and left home. I started preaching when I was eleven [and preached] till I was thirteen years old. You see, I was raised in the Holy Sanctified Church, and that church had very strict rules. You were either a hypocrite or you were not, either a sinner or not, either saved or not. This little girl was about seventeen, and she was my first experience.

How would you describe the type of boy you were—shy, bold, a show-off?
I was a typical little boy, not shy. I had to fight a lot, because kids used to make fun of me and my clothes. I didn't have decent clothes to wear to school, and I used to fight a lot if kids made fun of me in front of girls. That's the way we grew up, fighting. I started going to the gym in 1946, and I started boxing as a sparring partner, and hanging around and getting beat on for a couple of hours at the 12th Street Y. In high school, I played a little football, but I left school, trying to get a little experience in life. I didn't play any more piano, but I did go back home every now and then to give my mother and stepfather some money and to make sure that they knew I was all right. I was trying to make it on my own. We were very poor, and I didn't want to be a burden. I believed in God. I still do, but, then, I didn't have much choice. I stayed in the church, and I was very religiously inclined.

Many of your songs and grooves contain the evidence of folklore in them. Do you carry stories, slang, bits and pieces of conversations, and gossip around inside of you?

I grew up around a lot of older people, and I hung with a lot of older guys, and they used to tell me a lot of stories about their lives. I left home at such a young age, I had to hobo. I was homeless. I caught freight trains and boxcars, and I stayed and slept where I could, but I always managed to get a job. I made myself look older so that I could get a job during school hours. Because, in those days, they weren't hiring kids who didn't go to school. I was lucky enough to get a few night jobs and a few day jobs surviving any way that I could. But, as time went on, I began to get in trouble, and I ended up incarcerated—several times—and the only thing I learned about those first jails that I went to was how not to go to those same jails again. But when I went to Lorton Reformatory, in Lorton, Virginia, I found myself and learned how to play guitar. That was 1959 to '60, and in 1962, I got out. A young man in Lorton made my first guitar. He made it for five cartons of cigarettes. Lorton is a place of education and rehabilitation. Fats made my first guitar, but there was another guy who made guitars better than him, and his name was Bill Walker.

On "Bustin' Loose," you call, "I say, 'Shall I?' " and the band responds, "Roach 'em on down!" What does "Roach 'em on down" mean?

Roach 'em on down—you understand, when you smoke the joint down to a roach, and then you take that, and you—[*laughs*]—roach 'em down. You finish it up. But I really didn't want to talk about that. We smoked a little herb back in those days. We used to get down to the roach, understand.

George Clinton says that Funkadelic simply sped the blues up to discover its brand of funk. How did you decide to slow funk down and to incorporate the percussive bridge between grooves?

I grew up with the blues. When I was a child, that's all they used to play on the radio, and there was somebody sitting outside playing it too. Everybody in my family could play something: harmonica, guitar, accordion, or something. My mother played accordion, blew harmonica, and she played a little piano. My mother could sing, man. She was so talented that she had offers in the 1940s and the late 1930s. They wanted her to record blues and jazz, but she was so religious, she refused. "No, I don't sing nothing but God, and I don't sing for nobody but God." She didn't want to cut records or any of that. She just wanted to sing church. That's where my talent comes from.

A lot of blues are slow. I put "Stormy Monday" above a go-go feel, up-tempo, so people could dance to it. A lot of the tunes that we used to do back when I was doing Top 40, we slowed down. We used to do twenty-five or thirty songs a night. Then we slowed them down and did less songs and started dropping that percussion in between; and the percussion came from the churches that I grew up in. When disco was out and flying a hundred beats a minute, I cut it in half onstage. I was looking for a sound, and it ended up being a sound for the town, because most of the bands jumped on it—that same church beat and a little bit of "Mister Magic" by Grover Washington, Jr. Every hit song that came on the radio, we had to do it. And if you didn't do James Brown, two chances to one, you wouldn't get that gig again. When it came to soul and energy and feel, James Brown was my biggest inspiration. Nobody did it like he did it. I used to do all of his hits, and I think we did them very well. There were a lot of James Brown imitators, but I wasn't trying to imitate him. I was just doing his tunes to make people dance.

The original Soul Searchers are D.C. legends, the transitional blueprint from funk to go-go. What was that journey like, becoming a Soul Searcher and creating go-go?

I used to play with a group called Los Latinos, and that's where I really got my experience, because we only had four instruments: my guitar, John Euell's bass, Thomas Smith's congas, and Joe Manley's timbales. We didn't have horns, keyboards, or trap drums, which is why I left. I wanted a drummer. It was Joe Manley's band, and, at my suggestion, we later added Lloyd Pinchback on flute. I had to play the Top 40 tunes on my guitar. I had to find those chords, and I had to learn those changes, and it wasn't easy work, but it was fun. We weren't making any money either, but when I started doing the groove, I stopped doing a whole lot of Top 40. I put that groove in the middle. When I left Los Latinos to form my own band, that percussion was the dominant factor in what I wanted to do. At the time that I discovered the new sound, the Young Senators—another very popular local band—were away working with Eddie Kendricks, and they might have made the transition to go-go, but they never came back. A lot of groups did that—went on the road and never came back.

While the Soul Searchers were away doing *Soul Train* and touring, other bands such as Trouble, Rare Essence, and Experience Unlimited did make the transition from Top 40 to go-go. What was the scene like when you got back?

D.C. has the last say-so, but if you leave and stay too long, they don't like that. Local fans don't appreciate that. If you stay away too long, you often have to rebuild yourself or come out with another hit record or something, hoping and praying that they like it. I never even thought about going away and

staying. We did stay too long one time—a little more than a year when "Bustin' Loose" came out, traveling all over the country. When we got back, the acceptance was great, but it wasn't what it was before we left, and most of the bands were doing our sound.

I imagine that it wasn't easy for the groove to catch on. Even your own early singles were dance-track fast, and I believe that the go-go was mentioned for the first time on "Blow Your Whistle," which was recently sampled by Eve.
Go-go started catching on in 1976, and I was working with it in 1972 when I put out *We the People*. We were playing six nights a week around the city and some nights we'd have little fights, and I would get on the mic and say little rhymes like *When-are-we-the-people-going to-be-able-to-see-it together, together. Loving-one-another-can-be-easier-than-lifting a feather, a feather. Now if you can love your brother, hey, your brother can love another, hey, whenever-we-the-people-understand-one-another, we-the-people-can-love-each-other, wow!* You didn't have no hair on your face when that came out. I love messages. I didn't want nobody coming to the go-go fighting and raising Cain. Just love each other and have fun. That's what it was about, but the go-go hadn't caught on yet, because "We the People" was up-tempo. I put out "Blow Your Whistle" right after that, and kids were riding bicycles, shaking their tambourines, and blowing whistles, coming to the go-go like that.

Talk specifically about the strengths of the original Soul Searchers and how "Bustin' Loose" changed your life.
"Bustin' Loose" went national because the Soul Searchers were a hell of a band. The front cover and the back cover of the album [1979's *Bustin' Loose*] was done by the record company, and I appreciated everything they did for our sound. The conga pocket that started it all was played by Gregory "Bright Moments" Gerran. And he was a good listener and could play whatever beat you wanted, but, after about a year, he left and went with Gil Scott-Heron. There was John Buchanan who graduated from Notre Dame, and he was a very sharp music teacher, which was very important, because I didn't read music—it has to be *feel*. So I hired him maybe five years after I put the band together as a trombone player, because he had some great ideas about how to enhance our sound. The band sounded fatter, thanks to him. Donald Tillery, an amazing trumpet player with chops that no one in D.C. could top, could hit the highest notes, solo very well, and he could arrange. He started all of that screaming that other trumpet players in the area like Little Benny and them used to do at the end of the bridge. My main man,

Leroy Fleming, used to play with the Young Senators, but they were on the road a lot, and Leroy wanted to stay home and play. He was a great horn man: very soulful solos, full of ideas, and he looked great up there—very photogenic, tall, and cool. He had great stage presence. Le Ron Young, another special musician, played guitar on "Could It Be Love." And then there was Skip Fennell, a blind cat on keyboards, a Stevie Wonder man. I'm talking about Stevie Wonderful—so much soul. He's the one playing all that funky piano you hear back there. Curtis Johnson, who played the Hammond B-3 organ, was with us for a couple of years. Then he left and came back. That's him on "If It Ain't Funky." Jerry Wilder, the baddest bass player in the city at that time, stayed with us about a year or two. Nobody quits this band. When you mess up with me—well, it takes three or four times, and then I am going to miss you. When you get a hit record, you got to watch and see whose head blows up; and that's what I do, and when I see that, okay. Ricardo Wellman, that's my boy, Sugar Foot. His daddy was my first drummer in 1966: Frank Wellman. We played at the Pitts Red Carpet Lounge. We played at the Ebony Inn. And Marion Barry used to come to the Pitts Red Carpet Lounge—[located in the Pitts] Motor Hotel on Belmont Street, N.W. It was a beautiful place, one of the exclusive Black hotels in the city. Nat King Cole stayed there. Billy Eckstine and Sarah Vaughn stayed there. Sugar Foot was bad, still is, and he played exactly what you told him to play. I coordinated "Bustin' Loose." I put together every beat on that record, every horn lick, every guitar strut, everything, and Ricky just made the whole thing happen. After he left me, he went with Miles Davis for about four or five years, but when Miles came off the road, he came back to me.

Where did the term "go-go," as a name for the D.C. groove, come from?
They had go-go clubs and go-go girls, so I decided to call this music go-go music, because it just keeps going and going. At first, I didn't know what to call it. All I knew is that I wanted to put that Latin African feel in there and drop that tempo and add that percussion, some call-and-response, and communicate back and forth with the crowd. When it first started catching on, we were playing at the Maverick Room off of Rhode Island Avenue, N.E. It had tables and chairs, and folks all dressed nice. But when we started hitting that go-go groove, next week, those table and chairs disappeared, and the coats were all on the floor, and everybody was dancing. No more sitting down like at a cabaret waiting for everybody to get drunk to dance. They started dancing on the first beat, and next thing you know, they ain't dressing up no more—coming to party now—and younger people started coming, more and more. And then it got to be like the Soul Searchers were the Pied Piper: everywhere you look, the crowd was following us everywhere. It really felt good. And it was the most exciting thing that ever happened to me. And then when the other bands started picking up on the groove, that really made me feel good, as long as nobody didn't try to claim it. That happened a couple of times, but the fans got on the radio and straightened that out. I didn't have to say that I was the Godfather. They said it. My fans said it. I didn't have to proclaim this title for myself. D.C. did it, because D.C. knows what's up. They know who started what.

They certainly know the pocket, and you can't have go-go without the pocket and its various gears and exchanges between the drums and congas. Do you have any rules for the pocket, especially given all the new styles of go-go such as bounce beat and crank?
My rule for the pocket is to lock. You lock that pocket, and you keep going. The drummer and the conga player are the hardest-working men in the band. Once they lock that pocket, that's something you can't resist. A lot of groups haven't caught on to that part yet. But most of the groups here in Washington that play go-go got that percussion pocket locked. I've got to give them credit. Most of them have their own sound, which is cool, and some of them sound just like all the other bands, which is not cool. So you have to develop your own style, which is what I did with go-go, because I sounded like everybody else when I was playing Top 40. Then, when we learned how to lock that pocket in the socket, I said, "Damn, this is better than the music itself, and it just goes and goes and goes, and it got to be funky." Take the Junkyard Band, for instance. That was the funkiest little group I ever heard. And they came up playing on buckets and tin cans, and you couldn't resist the feeling of it. Wink and Heavy One, they sounded like no one else. Yes indeed, oh yeah, Lincoln Ross was also on "Bustin' Loose." He played trombone. Matter of fact, John Buchanan was not on "Bustin' Loose." He was late getting to the studio, and we had finished the song before he got there. I hired him to play trombone, but Stevie Wonder gave him keyboards. He was very experimental.

The release of 1986's *Go-Go Swing Live* changed the game. It brought the live P.A. sound to store-sold go-go recordings and kind of glorified the bootleg. How did that happen?
On *Go-Go Swing*, we had a good engineer, Reo Edwards. That's right—the man who wore shades at night at the Club LeBaron. That's how we got that live energetic sound and stu-

dio quality together. He could really mix sound. We recorded that at Crystal Skate. *Dowop dowop dowop*. I used to hum that when I was a kid—*Don't mean a thing, if you ain't got that swing*—so I decided to hook it up to a go-go beat. If you can get that groove up under there, two chances to one, it'll work. Reo was my manager, and he also managed Trouble Funk, and he didn't want no whole lot of credit. He just wanted people to recognize what was making the band sound good. He was very sharp. He knew how to make things sharp and how to carry sound from one dimension to another. *Go-Go Swing* was clean. You remember when I used to tell the kids to *follow your orders and bring your recorders*? Remember, y'all used to run around with the boom boxes up on y'all shoulders? And now those bootlegs are all over the world on labels I haven't heard of— fake, fake, fake—with some picture of me from the Internet, and folks still buying them. Record stores are catching hell over this, and so am I.

A lot of go-go bands have backed hip-hop artists and received zero credit. I was in the Howard Theater waiting to hear Rare Essence the first time I heard "Rapper's Delight." Did hip-hop steal go-go's shine?

A talker is different from a rapper, and my main man right now is Big G of the Backyard Band. That's the man right now. Little Benny and James Funk were great too. I also produced the first Rare Essence record, "Body Moves," and I used to go to their rehearsals over on Xenia Street and at Cheriy's and give them pointers, and [I went] to Backyard rehearsals years ago. Feeling the crowd, saying things they want to hear, allowing them to repeat after you are all important parts of knowing the people and being a part of them. Getting them pumped up and into your show are also things that make a good talker. That's the way it's done, live. There's a tremendous difference between talking and rapping. Rap is rhyming. A talker is not as controlled as a rapper. A talker's more natural. Rappers tell stories. I love rap—positive rap. I don't like that raw stuff. Even when I was young, I didn't like to hear someone talking raw on the microphone. I love hip-hop, but go-go is about the vibe. The vibe and the energy are the story. When you cranking, that means you are hyped, and when you grooving, that means you are laid back. I like to groove, and my hype man, Little Benny, cranks it up. I raised him, and he comes in and hits you. Benny is full of fun and loves new ideas. He has amazing stage presence, and, just like Tillery, he can blow two trumpets at once and play the tambourine. Benny's got a lot of Tillery in him, and couldn't nobody play every inch of the tambourine like Tillery. He was one of the pioneers of this business.

For about fifteen years, the inner city belonged to go-go and was decorated so with Day-Glo posters announcing shows; then the city outlawed them, passing out fines to clubs and management for promoting that way, pushing go-go further underground with its efforts to gentrify D.C.

We put the fans on the cover of *Go-Go Swing* to make it look like, a little like, a go-go poster. Max Kidd was one of the best promoters of go-go. He did a lot of great things for go-go, and Roy Benn was a great poster man. You could ride down the Beltway and see one in the middle of the underpass and wonder how it got there. Roy did it. He was from Jamaica, and they used to look good on the telegraph poles. Then at one point, I got tired of seeing that, so I told all the promoters, "Don't put me up on no more posters, or on nobody's windows or trees," 'cause I wanted them to put me on the radio! That's another cheap way of getting off. Do me some radio. Plus, it's hard work for the person who was hanging them, but the posters did reach the kids. Y'all used to take them down too, but after a while, I just got tired of seeing my face up there. I didn't mind what the other bands did.

Go-go will be forever framed and judged by the challenge of going national. Having left and come back, what are your thoughts on this?

Go-go has gone national. I mean, it is national. It's not as explosive as rap, but it has gone national. I can't name all the places, but they play it in Europe, Japan, and Zurich, Switzerland. They play it in Russia, and they have a station in Germany that plays go-go all day and night. Go-go is a survivor with its own style and excitement. It even survived all those damn bullets and those tough times here in the 1980s and 1990s by always incorporating music into the groove. It didn't just go *bloop bloop bidoop boopboop* all night. I mean the kids love that, but they also want some music too. They're young, and they rush, and there's no foreplay in the groove anymore. I used to start with ballads, and now we don't even do ballads anymore. I use the "Love Theme from the Godfather" now, and that's mellow, but when I hit the stage, everybody's on me with: "Wind me up, Chuck!" And I can't get warmed up, so sometimes I refuse the hype. I may get into it and holler with them, then I break it down and bring it back up, slow. I tried to do that at the Rock and Roll Hall of Fame, but I couldn't hear a thing in there.

But the bullets did take their toll on D.C. and on go-go. I remember Quentin "Footz" Davidson, the late, great Rare Essence founder and drummer. That was James Funk's brother. Funk knew how to talk and how to pump a crowd up, and Footz was right on his butt, him and Jungle Boogie and Mickey. They had a natural communication, and with Funky Ned on bass—whew! That was a tight band and a great unit—even Redds (rest in peace) when he was with them, on guitar. He was a funny guy and had so much soul. The young'uns don't know much about Redds with Essence or with Redds and the Boys. We used to call Rare Essence the Baby Soul Searchers, but they couldn't last together, [with] all those greats and personalities in one band, egos. All musicians need ego, confidence in themselves. Remember "Umm-Umm Good"? After I fired my whole band, I gave that cut to Essence, but they didn't have anyone who could sing it, so I sang it with them.

The sound ain't always worth the egos. Musicians always change when the band gets popular. I don't change. I stayed humble, and I'm nice to all of my fans, and I pay my musicians well. And I'm good at picking replacements, and the replacement doesn't have to be as talented as the person he or she is replacing, as long as he or she has a good personality. I'm more humble than I was when I started, and I don't intimidate people anymore. Back in the day, I used to be very intimidating. I was tough. You couldn't look at me wrong. You play that good music and that was it; get your money and God bless you.

That's ironic because you are known for your signature laugh and love of hats. When did that begin?

My mother bought my first hat when I was about six years old. I thought I was a little man, and, back in the '50s, I wore Dobbs and Knox, and Stacy Adams shoes. You had to have a hat, else you wasn't hip. Young boys fourteen and fifteen years old had to have that hat. I've been wearing hats my whole life, and at a show, I'm 'a hit you with a full meal, many styles of hats: fatback, ham hocks, collard greens, black-eyed peas, and lima beans. That's what you get here. My current band is younger, more energetic. I share the spotlight more now. I'm an old man now, and I love giving young people a break: Little Benny, KK (my daughter) who raps on "Chuck Baby," Sweet Cherie (keyboards), and Ju Ju (my drummer), he's top dog. Him and Mighty Moe (congas) are the hardest-working men in the band. I raised Ju Ju too; took him all over Europe with me. My producer Chucky Thompson, too, I also raised him. He lied to me about his age and come find out he was seventeen or so when we went to Europe, but he had so much talent—one of the baddest producer cats I've ever worked with. He's very responsible for our new sound. That's him with me, Mafioso style, on the cover of *We're About the Business*. All of them grew up wanting to play with me. The Godfather raised them all.

At the beginning of 2007's *We're About the Business*, you make a bold claim about who runs D.C. At your age, can you back those claims up, and is being the "Godfather of Go-Go" enough for Chuck Brown?

This is Chuck Town, man. I didn't say it, the fans said it. And you can't go wrong with the fans. I am proud to have been recognized by the Rock and Roll Hall of Fame, even if I am never inducted. It is an honor to have my guitar there. I gave guitars to the Rock and Roll Hall of Fame, to the Smithsonian Institute, and the Library of Congress. It feels good to be the oldest person in go-go. I am grateful, and all of my strength and stamina come from the grace of God, my wife, Jocelyn Brown, "Ja Ja," a Sagittarius born in D.C., and from my kids. She had a crush on me when she was fourteen years old, and I said, "Girl you ain't old enough, so we're going wait a few years for you." And then when she turned twenty-one, I went back and got her. I said, "All right, you ready now?" We got four kids now and three grandchildren. About a year after we got together, I proposed. I remember exactly where I was when I proposed too. Can I say it? In bed! Being the "Godfather of Go-Go" is more than enough for me. In the beginning, I had a hard time trying to get certain band members to play go-go. One drummer said, "Man, I don't want to play that little stupid beat; ain't nothing but noise." I said, "But we got music incorporated into the groove." I had to change several drummers and band members in order to get to the go-go. "I got fast, slick hands," a drummer who had been with me for five years said. And I said, "I want something thumpin', some bottom. I don't need fast hands. I don't need nothing but snare, foot, and cymbals." A crash and a sock, that's all I need. The crash and a sock and a foot. A nice hard-stomping foot. ○

For more info on Chuck Brown, visit windmeupchuck.com.

GRAB ONE
BEFORE THEY'RE ALL GONE

CHECK OUT AT WWW.HHV.DE

CLOTHING, MUSIC, SNEAKERS, BOOKS & MAGAZINES
LIMITED ONES & ESSENTIALS WWW.HHV.DE

MORE THAN 75 000 ITEMS IN STOCK
CHECK OUT HHV.DE

AFRICA UNITE

JOIN THE MARLEY FAMILY FOR A CELEBRATION OF BOB'S VISION

CONCERT TRIBUTE, MARLEY FAMILY TRAVELOGUE, AND HUMANITARIAN DOCUMENTARY... THE FILM *AFRICA UNITE* IGNITES THE SCREEN WITH THE SPIRIT OF BOB MARLEY!

SPECIAL FEATURES INCLUDE:
- OVER 50 MINS OF COMPLETE CONCERT PERFORMANCES BY THE MARLEY FAMILY & FRIENDS, INCLUDING FAVORITES "I SHOT THE SHERIFF," "JAMMIN'," & "REBEL MUSIC"
- INTERVIEWS WITH THE MARLEY FAMILY
- ARCHIVAL BOB MARLEY FOOTAGE, NEW YORK CITY, CIRCA 1980

 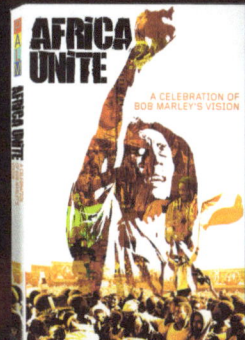

AVAILABLE ON DVD

"AFRICA UNITE... FOR IT'S LATER THAN YOU THINK." - BOB MARLEY

WWW.BOBMARLEY.COM/AFRICA UNITE

BORDERS

WHAT IT REALLY IS

Cleveland's S.O.U.L. sets the record straight

text James Steiner

Larry Hancock, who lent his warm, Bobby Bland–like baritone to S.O.U.L.'s 1973 full-length *Can You Feel It*, knows a little bit about this music thing. Like many singers of his generation, Hancock was born into a musical family, and many of his earliest memories involve sitting in on the rehearsals of his family's gospel group, Bed-Stuy's Gospel Messengers. But unlike so many of his contemporaries, Larry was first attracted to music not for its sound but for its *feel*. "At their rehearsals," he remembers, "my father would just sit me on top of the piano, and I would just *feel* it, you know? Just take it all in. And I would feel all those chords resonate underneath me—shaking me."

Sometimes, our senses can surprise us; and decades after Larry made his mark on soul music history with *Can You Feel It*, young vinyl addicts, amongst them luminaries like Pete Rock and Large Professor, would discover the music of S.O.U.L. through a similar type of synesthetic magic. Where young Larry Hancock was able to feel the sounds made by the Gospel Messengers, aspiring beatmakers flipping through piles of dusty vinyl were able to see the promise of funky grooves in the covers of S.O.U.L.'s two records, *What Is It* and *Can You Feel It*. Though they were pressed on Musicor, a label better known for country and pop hits from the likes of George Jones and Gene Pitney, the cool reserve exuded by the solemn-faced, nattily dressed young men on the covers carried with it enough promise to entice young diggers to take the records home.

Thankfully, S.O.U.L.'s music more than delivered upon the extravagant promises of those covers, and the tracks that sampled the propulsive beat of tracks like "Peace of Mind" and a cover of "Burning Spear" lived up to the greatness of their source materials. But while S.O.U.L. may have gained fame amongst hip-hop fanatics for the breaks that form the basis of classics like Main Source's "Peace Is Not the Word to Play" and Pete Rock and C.L. Smooth's "Go with the Flow," the music they made between 1971 and 1974 is far more than mere sample fodder. Anchored by the metronome-steady drumming of Paul Stubblefield, S.O.U.L. turned soul standards into genre-defying excursions into the unknown and composed bracing original material that left their hometown audiences wanting more.

Larry Hancock and S.O.U.L.'s multitalented bandleader Gus Hawkins remember their tenures in the nascent Cleveland soul scene of the mid-'60s—basement rehearsals and local talent contests—their trial-by-fire residency at the Apollo Theater, and the group's eventual dissolution in late 1974.

"I got into music through my family's gospel and through my Uncle Louie, a pianist," remembers Larry Hancock. "He wasn't famous, like a lot of those guys, but he was a very sharp dresser; he was one of the most elegant dressers I've ever seen in my life, and, well, that made me say, 'When I grow up, I wanna be like Uncle Louie.'" It might have been Uncle Louie's influence that drew Larry away from his family's gospel and toward secular music. "Eventually, I turned into a rebel. My folks really wanted me to stay with gospel, but, back in them days, I was listening to the radio a lot, and what I was hearing really spoke to me. And I told my folks, 'This is not the devil's music; it may sound different to you, but it really comes from God.' I was always conscious of the musical and lyrical continuity [between gospel and soul]."

Larry's family soon relocated from Bed-Stuy to Cleveland, and his restlessness would cause him to begin exploring Cleveland's soul scene at a young age. "I'd put some of my mama's eyeliner on my lip, make a little mustache, and make like I was twenty-one to sneak into the clubs. [*laughs*] I met a lot of these cats then." Amongst the veteran Cleveland sidemen who made their living backing up the big-name acts that would stop through was a young Gus Hawkins. To this day, Larry speaks of Gus with the reverence and affection of a younger sibling: "He's been like a big brother to me. Before I even met him, I'd watch Gus from the stage when he was playing with all these guys. He played behind big-time groups—the Temptations, Aretha Franklin, Wilson Pickett, Chuck Jackson, Gene Chandler. I finally met Gus when I was about fifteen. I had been singing around a bit, and when it came time to record my very first record, 'I've Got to Find Myself a Girl,' he was the sax player. I tell you, at that time, I felt like I had arrived! Just getting a chance to play with Gus was a real honor."

Gus Hawkins was born into a family of Alabama sharecroppers, and followed them north to the Cleveland suburbs at the age of four. He'd honed his chops in his high school marching band, and, like Larry, he had fallen in love with the sounds he'd heard broadcast by the local soul station, WABQ. So when he was offered a spot playing sax with the Futuretones, a hot local act with a fiery lead singer by the name of

Sounds of Unity and Love
photo courtesy of Dante Carfagna

Charles Edwin Hatcher, he jumped at the chance. The Futuretones built up quite a reputation through a rigorous gigging schedule, and their charismatic singer eventually caught the eye of Bill "Honky Tonk" Doggett, who offered to take him to Detroit for an audition with Motown. Gus remembers: "I was supposed to go to Motown too. Charles got with him 'cause Bill [Doggett] needed a lead singer, and he also needed a tenor player. But I got cold feet, you know. I was only seventeen and had never left home."

Though Charles Hatcher's audition with Motown failed to pan out at first, he did return to Cleveland with a deal with Ed Wingate's Ric Tic Records, and a new name: *Edwin Starr*. Looking to cut a distinctive debut single, Starr roped Gus into a group, the Soul Agents, made up of veteran Cleveland sidemen and a couple of Detroit players, a ferocious guitar slinger named Anthony Hawkins and drummer Tyrone Hite. The record they cut together, "Agent Double-O Soul," hit the R&B top ten in 1965. The song is remarkable for its uncompromising ferocity, which displayed both the tightly wound discipline that would come to characterize Gus Hawkins's work with S.O.U.L., and the amp-busting roar that would eventually find its way into Anthony Hawkins and Tyrone Hite's psychedelic funk outfit, Black Merda. It's a testament to the creative fecundity of the Midwestern soul scene that a song as simple, but powerful, as "Agent Double-O Soul" could eventually lead to the creation of two such inspired, yet stylistically divergent groups.

Though Edwin's commercial success would eventually cause him to abandon the Soul Agents, the experience that Gus Hawkins earned in that outfit would inspire him with the confidence to strike out on his own. After a trying tenure as a medic in Vietnam, Gus returned to Cleveland to form a group that was strikingly different from any that he had played in before. Gus remembers: "When I came home, that's when I hooked up with [bassist] Lee [Lovett] and [guitarist] Walter Winston, who had a group called the Dynamic Sounds. They were doin' this little club gig on Friday and Saturday nights. I got to playin' with them, then later I got Paul [Stubblefield] to come and play drums, and hired his brother Vic, who had also been playing trumpet with Edwin Starr."

Like many local bands, they pleased the crowd with renditions of contemporary soul hits, but Gus, always an ambitious arranger, put his own stamp on tunes like the Temptations' "Message From a Black Man," Donny Hathaway's "The Ghetto," and Richard Evans's "Burning Spear," stripping them down to spacious rhythmic workouts and leaving room for improvisational interplay. The Dynamic Sounds' adventurous arrangements would win them many local followers. Gus recalls how one day in 1970 "somebody said they got this contest goin' on for a TV program, and you'd win a thousand dollars and a record deal with a record com-

"Pee Wee" Winston, Paul Stubblefield, Gus Hawkins's aunt Mae Frances, Gus, and Lee Lovett at a gig in Cleveland
photo courtesy of Gus Hawkins

S.O.U.L.

pany in New York. So we entered the contest, and we beat out all the bands—gained first place. Art Talmudge came down from Musicor Records to sign us." On arriving in New York to cut their first single, a radical reinterpretation of Donny Hathaway's "The Ghetto" entitled "Down in the Ghetto," Art Talmudge requested that the band change their name. In a moment of inspiration, Gus came up with the acronym S.O.U.L., short for Sounds of Unity and Love.

"Down in the Ghetto" was enough of a success on the Cleveland market to convince Musicor to offer S.O.U.L. a five-year contract and an opportunity to return to New York to cut a full LP. But the ailing label had little experience, and even less interest, in marketing R&B groups. A dusty photo of the Jackson 5, whom Musicor had been foolish enough to drop before their eventual ascent to stardom with Barry Gordy, hung neglected in the Musicor offices, and was Gus's first clue that something was amiss at the troubled label. According to Gus, "They wouldn't spend no money on anybody. They didn't know how to market or nothing! They simply didn't have anything together." Musicor's incompetence and indifference would put a significant strain on the sessions for S.O.U.L.'s first full-length: "They made us work so fast, and we didn't have any [original] material." Gus remarks with an ironic chuckle, "The only thing we had was that song 'S.O.U.L.' Everything was rush, rush, rush. I was never satisfied."

As a final insult, the clueless Musicor failed to comprehend the title that Gus proposed for the album, *What It Is*, which Musicor tellingly changed to *What Is It*, a phrase that neatly describes Musicor's complete failure to recognize the treasure they had uncovered in S.O.U.L. Despite these setbacks, 1971's *What Is It* stands as a remarkable document of S.O.U.L.'s incendiary musicianship. If anything, the rushed nature of these recordings adds an edge of inspired urgency that gives *What Is It* the electrifying energy of a live performance.

Determined to cut S.O.U.L.'s second record on his own terms, Gus set about restructuring the group and writing original material. While both Gus and Lee Lovett had performed some vocal turns on *What Is It*, Gus realized that the band needed a charismatic vocalist to take S.O.U.L. to the next level. After a little thought, Gus remembered Larry Hancock, the shy but gifted young singer with whom he had cut "I Got to Find Myself a Girl" years before. When Larry, who had just returned from a stint in the Army, got the call, he was elated.

Larry recalls, "When he asked me to join, I just said, 'Man, I don't think I got the chops.' I wasn't that confident in myself at twenty-two. Everything was happening so fast, coming home from the service, and then about six months later being asked to join a national recording group. I was a little young whippersnapper. I mean, this was a professional job; I'd done a few little things but never something of this magnitude. After I joined, we went straight to rehearsing. As a matter of fact, we went underground for about nine months just getting our set together."

By the time that S.O.U.L. returned to New York to cut their second album, *Can You Feel It*, they had assembled a formidable repertoire of original material, including "Peace of Mind," with its rough-hewn central horn riff, and the storming "Tell It Like It Is," which plays like a raucous hybrid of the Temptations' Whitfield-produced psychedelic soul and Funkadelic's righteously unhinged early work. However, S.O.U.L. once again encountered troubles with Musicor, who could only spare them studio time while they were in the midst of a grueling residency at Harlem's Apollo Theater. The shows were a triumph—Larry remembers receiving standing ovations every night—but Gus once again felt that S.O.U.L. was being undermined by the hapless and apathetic Musicor.

"We were [at the Apollo] from twelve in the afternoon to midnight," Gus recalls. "Then at seven in the morning, we gotta be in the studio again! Therefore, I never thought that we did our best. We couldn't do our best. You can't do your best like that. You know how long it takes people to do albums? Years, sometimes! But we felt that with the material we had, it would be great. We're gonna be able to take more time and really express where we're coming from now. We could never do that before. 'Cause it was always on somebody else's time and their terms. And they're not us, so they don't feel what we're feeling. And, 'cause they're paying for everything, they don't give a damn how tired you are. That was very hard and strenuous doing *Can You Feel It*."

Listening to the precise arrangements, close harmonies, and expansive percussion of *Can You Feel It*, it's difficult to detect evidence of the immense strain of which Gus speaks. The band sounds confident and assured as they work their way through the late-night soul of Larry Hancock's "To Mend a Broken Heart" and the snappy Booker T.–evoking grooves of "Do Whatever You Want to Do."

Can You Feel It clearly saw S.O.U.L. on the verge of a major creative breakthrough, but their considerable promise would remain unfulfilled. Though the group would begin to work on sessions for an unreleased third album, they were unable to secure possession of the masters for it when they left Musicor in 1974, and only one track, the frenetic junkie lament "The Joneses," would ever see release. In the wake of this disappointment, the band split up on New Year's Eve 1974. Gus and Larry remain close to this day and, thanks to a resurgence of interest in S.O.U.L, continue to draw appreciative audiences in Cleveland. Though Gus speaks somewhat ruefully of missed opportunities, few could ask for a more rewarding legacy than S.O.U.L.'s small but powerful body of work, which continues to inspire musicians and producers to this day. ●

waxpoetics

"THIS COMPILATION OF 'FAVORITE' ARTICLES FROM THE HARD-TO-FIND MAGAZINE'S FIRST FIVE ISSUES IS A MUST-HAVE FOR ANYONE WITH A DEEP INTEREST IN AMERICAN MUSIC AND THE CULTURE SURROUNDING IT."
–*Publisher's Weekly* (starred review)

"A COFEE-TABLE-READY COLLECTION OF ALBUM COVERS, FROM THE LEWD TO THE LUDICROUS. IT'S PERFECT."
–*The Village Voice*

Wax Poetics Anthology, Volume 1 celebrates the magazine's early years (2001-2003) with a hardbound edition. Complete with new photographs and illustrations, we revisit articles on James Brown's drummers Clyde Stubblefield and Jab'O Starks, bassist Sweet Charles, and vocalist Marva Whitney; jazz genius Charles Mingus; funky drummers Idris Muhammad and Pretty Purdie; salsa giant Fania Records, reggae producers Clive Chin and King Tubby; golden-era hip-hop producers Prince Paul, Da Beatminers, Diamond D, and Wu-Tang's the RZA; films *Wild Style* and *Style Wars*; and breakbeat bootleg *Ultimate Breaks & Beats*.

Cover Story: Album Cover Art vividly explores an element of music culture that has withered with the advent of MP3s and digital downloading. Records possess a visual as well as aural capacity for storytelling. The record cover–eye candy for the music lover–speaks a language rooted in the environment and era of the music itself. And, more intimately, a record can create a profound sense of analogy with its owner, and it's this relationship that we share. All records handpicked by Wax Poetics contributers.

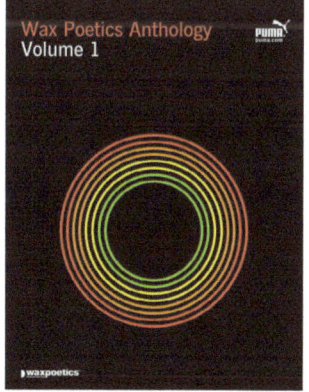
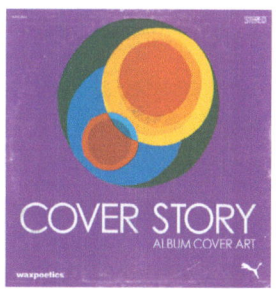

out now on wax poetics books

Masterpiece Theatre

American jazz legends make moving pictures abroad

text
Matt Rogers

photography
Michael Ochs Archives/Getty Images

Smooth jazz. Hints of groove canned for your non-listening pleasure, an oxymoronic genre that promises never to make you grimace. How the term has become synonymous with faux-funk dribble and slow "grown folks night" grind is a cultural crime. Point the finger at whomever you like, from the ubiquitous corporate takeover of urban radio to the once-upon-a-time-on-the-corner "hip" transformed into the now on-the-couch arthritic hips.

Which makes the Jazz Icons series, a hefty seven-DVD box set recently released by Reelin' in the Years Productions, all the more important. Whether you're rookie or connoisseur, the series (now in its second volume) brings smooth jazz booty for all. *Smooth jazz*, you say? Try Duke. Trane. Dexter. Not smooth enough for ya? How 'bout Sarah. Wes. Brubeck. Mingus. When it comes to *real* jazz, you simply *can't* get smoother (okay, maybe Mingus bucks the smooth moniker, but damn if he wasn't *sharp*). You get them all in this plush package, complete with copious liner notes, rare photos, and hours of heretofore unseen live footage. Six of these DVDs focus on each of these jazz giants (a seventh "bonus disc" contains extra performances), each precious not only for the audio feats contained within, but, more importantly, for giving us a glimpse as to *how* each of these jazz masters interacted with each other and their audiences (who, mind you, *dressed* when they went out).

Filmed in black and white between 1958 and '64, each disc provides a window into the genius of each artist at the height of his musical powers. We also get to aurally chew on the artistry of many heavyweight "sidemen" who buttress each show. From the late, great Oscar Peterson to Jaki Byard, Paul Desmond to McCoy Tyner, Elvin Jones to Eric Dolphy, Stan Getz to Johnny Hodges—all leaders in their own right—it simply does not get any better—smoother—than this.

Perhaps the best-filmed set of the series belongs to Dexter Gordon, as it clearly captures the cool, yet imposing, presence of the man. Watch Sarah Vaughn—her voice a maelstrom of force and beauty, her body tight like a tailback—shape-shift standards into brilliant terra incognita; witness Charles Mingus stretch his bass, literally and figuratively, with rapid-fire runs while "assisting" pianist Byard's solo by plucking his exposed piano strings; float with Dave Brubeck as he takes "Take Five" into the land of butter and honey; gasp as Wes Montgomery flings so many silky notes from his guitar while strumming merely with his thumb; wonder at John Coltrane as he effortlessly blows tunes that made him famous, like "My Favorite Things" and "Impressions"; and bear witness to how the Maestro, Duke Ellington, the epitome of charisma and class, guides his sixteen-piece big band through mini-suites that serve to remind that jazz *is* America's classical music.

You wanna know what all the fuss was about forty, fifty years ago? Grab these DVDs and give thanks once again to almighty Thor and them Northern Europeans, who not only had the insight to visually capture these jazz giants while still in their prime, but didn't toss the languishing tapes years later. Damn, does it always take an outsider to preserve one's culture?

www.ingramcontent.com/pod-product-compliance
Lightning Source LLC
Chambersburg PA
CBHW041701160426
43191CB00002B/48